Campbell River

Campbell River

Gateway to the Inside Passage
Including Strathcona, the Discovery Islands and the
Mainland Inlets

Ian Douglas
Photos by Boomer Jerritt

Harbour Publishing

BRITISH COLUMBIA

Port Hardy

Port McNeill

Woss

Sayward

Campbell River

Quatsino Sound

Knight Inlet

Bute Inlet

Tahsis

Powell River

Gold River

Courtenay

Comox

Kyuquot Sound

Strathcona Provincial Park

Gibsons

Nootka Sound

Port Alberni

Vancouver

PACIFIC

Tofino

Nanaimo

OCEAN

Ucluelet

Strait of Georgia

VANCOUVER ISLAND

Barkley Sound

Port Renfrew

Juan de Fuca Strait

Victoria

USA

West Thurlow Island

Johnstone Strait

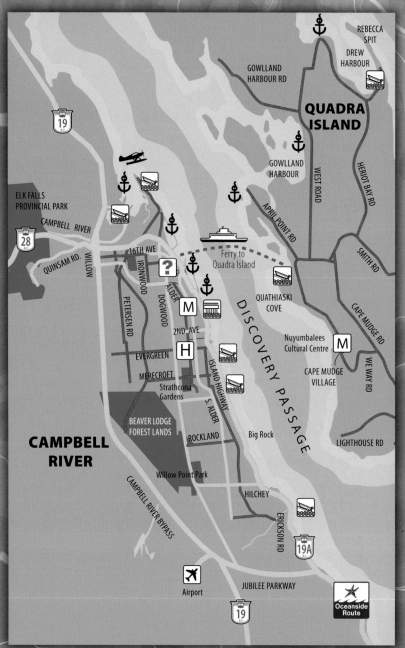

REBECCA SPIT

DREW HARBOUR

GOWLLAND HARBOUR RD

QUADRA ISLAND

GOWLLAND HARBOUR

WEST ROAD

HERIOT BAY RD

19

ELK FALLS PROVINCIAL PARK

CAMPBELL RIVER

28

APRIL POINT RD

SMITH RD

16TH AVE

QUINSAM RD.

WILLOW

IRONWOOD

?

Ferry to Quadra Island

DISCOVERY PASSAGE

QUATHIASKI COVE

CAPE MUDGE RD

Campbell Lake

PETERSEN RD

DOGWOOD

ALDER

M

2ND AVE

Nuyumbalees Cultural Centre

M

WE WAY RD

H

EVERGREEN

ISLAND HIGHWAY

CAPE MUDGE VILLAGE

MERECROFT

Strathcona Gardens

S. ALDER

CAMPBELL RIVER

BEAVER LODGE FOREST LANDS

ROCKLAND

Big Rock

LIGHTHOUSE RD

Willow Point Park

CAMPBELL RIVER BYPASS

HILCHEY

ERICKSON RD

19A

Upper Campbell Lake

Airport

JUBILEE PARKWAY

Oceanside Route

19

Up Quir Le

Strathcona Provincial Park

Buttle Lake

Page 1: A Campbell River tugboat, the workhorse of the coast, lies alongside in the fishing harbour waiting for its next tow.

Pages 2–3: Looking over Twin Islands and Kinghorn Island toward Desolation Sound and Mount Denman.

This spread: Fishing has changed from a year-round occupation to short openings with a fraction of the former fleet.

Pages 8–9: Campbell River is home to a mighty fleet of salmon seiners, many owned by First Nations families.

CONTENTS

Introduction:
A Wall of Islands

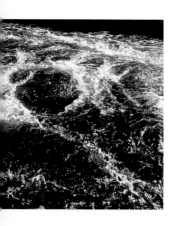

Above: The strong tidal currents forcing their way through the narrow passages between the Discovery Islands allow safe passage only at slack water.
Howard White photo

Right: Twilight descends upon the Campbell River fishing harbour and seawalk.

A fter unfolding in a northwesterly direction for 300 kilometres (185 miles), the great inland Salish Sea of British Columbia comes to an abrupt end in a wall of large islands at the 50th Parallel.

This obstruction was a disappointment to the early explorers, who held out hope that the Gulf of Georgia might lead into a marine highway that would provide a shortcut through the Americas, as the windy sixteenth-century sailor Juan de Fuca had led them to believe. The wall of islands did have gaps a ship could squeeze through but as the explorers soon discovered, they led farther up the western edge of the continental mass, not through it. Still, this was something, for the explorers themselves with their charting duties, for the First Nations who traversed the coast in their great war canoes, and for fur traders, settlers, Klondike gold rushers, sealers, arctic whalers, freighters, log booms, barges stacked with every imaginable cargo, generations of commercial salmon fishermen, pleasure boaters, cruise ships, Alaska commuters, and other assorted navigators of the Inside Passage who would follow in increasing numbers over the years. There were two main passages, one on the east against the mainland side and one on the west against the Vancouver Island shore. Both were made treacherous by the heavy tidal streams that came pouring down from the north, pinching between the islands in a frothing maelstrom of whirlpools and overfalls. The passage against the mainland side was narrower, twistier and more turbulent and was always less used than the passage on the Vancouver Island side, which was broader and shorter, though it made up for that with another sort of hazard, a dangerous reef called Ripple Rock that reared up in mid-passage and claimed the lives of more than one hundred mariners before it was finally

blasted out of existence by the world's largest non-nuclear peacetime explosion in 1958.

When the explorer George Vancouver approached the wall of islands, he chose the broader passage on the Island side, naming it Discovery Passage in recognition of both his purpose for being there and for his flagship, the HMS *Discovery*. Before advancing into the narrow passageway with its foaming bottleneck at Seymour Narrows, he wisely chose to anchor off the entrance and wait for a favourable tide, rest, refill his water casks, visit the local inhabitants and generally get into the right frame of mind to tackle the challenge of the upper coast. In so doing he anticipated the strategic value of the location that would someday become the gateway city of Campbell River, serving as both a northern terminus for the busy commerce of the gulf and as a staging place for forays into the "jungles" of the upper coast. The advantages of the location were not lost on First Nations, though at the time of Vancouver's arrival the only occupants were a peaceful band of 350 K'omoks Salish living atop the cliffs of Cape Mudge, the bouldery finger of Quadra Island that forms the eastern entrance to Discovery Passage. The K'omoks welcomed the Vancouver expedition and seemed disinclined to take advantage of their commanding position, but this was to change. Soon after Vancouver's voyage the more warlike Laichwiltach, a Kwakwaka'wakw tribe from the north, armed themselves with fur trade muskets and "raided and terrorized the Salish tribes along the Strait of Georgia… [and eventually] displaced the decimated Comox Indians of Cape Mudge and Campbell River" (Duff 1963). The invaders established two communities, the Wei Wai Kai on the Quadra side and the Wei Wai Kum on the Vancouver Island side. The Laichwiltach, also known as the Lekwiltok, Euclataw, or Yaculta, assumed a more typical role for a people who controlled a strategic pass and began exacting tribute from wayfarers, reacting with severity when they didn't get what they demanded.

Above: A fly fisherman plays a fish on the Campbell River, made famous by author Roderick Haig-Brown.

Below: Large cruise ships and powerful tugs towing chip barges must time their journey through the strong currents of Discovery Passage.

Previous pages: On June 23, 1946, a magnitude 7.2 earthquake caused part of Mount Colonel Foster to crash into Landslide Lake in Strathcona Provincial Park.

The territory commanded by the Laichwiltach, which roughly coincides with the area covered in this book, had much more going for it than just serving as a gateway. On the Vancouver Island side, there was the towering Elk River Mountain Range dominated by 2,201-metre (7,265-foot) Mount Golden Hinde, Vancouver Island's highest mountain, giving rise to one of the Island's largest rivers, the Campbell, which had a placid estuary protected by a large spit and a bountiful run of salmon. Across Discovery Passage began the chain of interlocking islands collectively called the Discovery Islands—Quadra, Read, Cortes, Sonora, the Thurlows and the Redondas—each with deeply indented shorelines and clam beaches suitable for supporting Native villages, most of which gave way in time to settlements occupied by European newcomers who gave them European names—Heriot Bay, Evans Bay, Mansons Landing, Whaletown, Owen Bay, Seaford, Thurlow, Big Bay, Deceit Bay and Refuge Cove. The Discovery Islands actually took the early lead in non-Native development with the establishment of a trading post on Cortes Island in the 1880s, a mine complete with townsite and two hotels on Thurlow Island in the 1890s, and a store, hotel, salmon cannery and settler population of two hundred on Quadra Island by 1910. Today the Discovery Islands remain sparsely populated and see mostly recreational use, except for Cortes and Quadra, which have significant year-round communities.

On the mainland side is a chain of fjords—Ramsey Arm, Frederick Arm, Phillips Arm, Loughborough Inlet and towering, formidable Bute Inlet. The upper Bute remained the domain of a Coast Salish tribe known as the Xwemalhkwu (Homalco), while two other Salish nations, the Klahoose and Sliammon, maintained summer encampments on some islands but by the mid-nineteenth century the rest of the territory was firmly in the possession of the Laichwiltach and their Kwakwaka'wakw kin to the north, who held sway over a vast archipelago clear to the northern extreme of Vancouver Island. As the great Kwakwaka'wakw civilization died down, a victim of

Top: First Nation memorial pole on the Cape Mudge reserve on Quadra Island.

Above: A backcountry skier prepares for a descent into the west bowl at the Mount Cain ski area north of Campbell River.

Right: The protected waters of the Discovery Islands draw kayakers from around the world.

Mansons Landing
Provincial Park is
named after Mike
Manson, who
started a trading
post near the First
Nation village site
of Clytosin in 1887.

To become a member of the world-famous Tyee Club you must catch a chinook salmon weighing at least 30 pounds from a rowboat in the waters of Discovery Passage.

whiteman's diseases and changing times, much of this watery world oriented itself toward the growing hub city of Campbell River, which emerged as the transportation, supply and social centre of the mid-coast region.

The first to seize upon Campbell River's potential in the modern era was a pair of Swedish immigrants named Charles and Frederick Thulin, whose original move in 1889 had been to found a small trading post and watering hole at a location they named Lund, which did good business fuelling and lubricating towboaters heading upcoast into the tidal passages of the mainland side. After a few years the enterprising Swedes realized they had a chance to completely monopolize traffic passing north-ward up the coast by duplicating their operation on the Vancouver Island side, where, in addition to a growing number of logging camps, there was the added attraction of a gentlemen's sportfishing boomlet developing around the mouth of the Campbell River. The Thulins bought 160 acres (65 hectares) including most of the present-day downtown for $800 and their Willows Hotel became a landmark, soon augmented by a store and that coastal equivalent of the railway station, a steamboat dock. The Thulin enterprise proved to be the seed of a commercial centre that grew rapidly, soon outstripping Lund, Quathiaski and every other settlement north of Nanaimo.

The Thulins were not entirely without the company of other non-Native settlers in their new neighbourhood, as the government had been encouraging settlers to take up land in the area for some years at a dollar an acre, and by 1901 there were 361 non-Native people living between Oyster River and Salmon River. Most were itiner-ant loggers, but a number were would-be agriculturists like the Nunnses, McIvors and Smiths who were bent upon "making these the British Isles of the West." As in other parts of BC, most early "stump ranchers" gave up wrestling their small homesteads from the forest as soon as they realized the forest itself was a far more valuable crop than anything they could plant to replace it. Once this realization fully set in, people began looking at the Campbell River area with different eyes.

For almost half a century the Elk Falls mill ran a sawmill, kraft and paper-making line that was the economic backbone of Campbell River.

Dating back to the days of the Laichwiltach it had been sought out because of its maritime advantages. Now its upland resources came into focus. Between the Oyster River drainage in the south and the Salmon River drainage in the north was a broad shelf of heavily forested land some 100 kilometres (60 miles) in length and 50 kilometres (30 miles) in width that supported one of the most valuable stands of prime Douglas fir timber on the coast. There were also minerals in this country, coal and metals that would eventually produce short-lived mines, but nothing rivalled the wealth of the area's timber. Lone handloggers discovered it first, using hand tools to take the tallest and straightest of the shore-side trees from the 1870s onward, but by the 1890s timber harvesting began on an epic scale as some of BC's largest operators set up shop in the territory. Hastings Mill, the leading forest company of the day, developed some of BC's first big railroad logging camps on Quadra and Thurlow islands and at Rock Bay in Johnstone Strait, eventually employing some 1,500 men in the area. The longest-running local firm, International Timber Company ("The Old I.T."), commenced logging within the present Campbell River townsite in 1906 and worked its way up the Campbell–Quinsam watersheds, changing its name to Elk River Timber (ERT) in 1929. The Laichwiltach, never slow to seize an advantage, learned the logging trade and started their own operations. Some of the province's legendary timber barons were drawn to the area—R.D. Merrill, P.B. Anderson and H.R. MacMillan. In 1922 J.B. Lamb opened his famous camp in Menzies Bay, affectionately known as "Daddy's Lamb's Ranch." Two other large railroad operations, Campbell River Timber Company and Bloedel, Stewart and Welch, also opened in the early 1920s, both with booming grounds in Menzies Bay. The Elk Falls Co. upped the ante in 1952 when it built the Duncan Bay pulp mill that would prosper and grow and serve as the area's leading employer until 2009, when depressed markets and a diminished wood supply forced it to close. By that time Campbell River boasted a population of over 30,000 and a full complement of urban amenities, making it the third-largest city on Vancouver Island.

Crossing the waters of Discovery Passage
on a spring morning, with Campbell
River's marine roots and forestry heritage
in full view, backed by snow-clad
mountains.

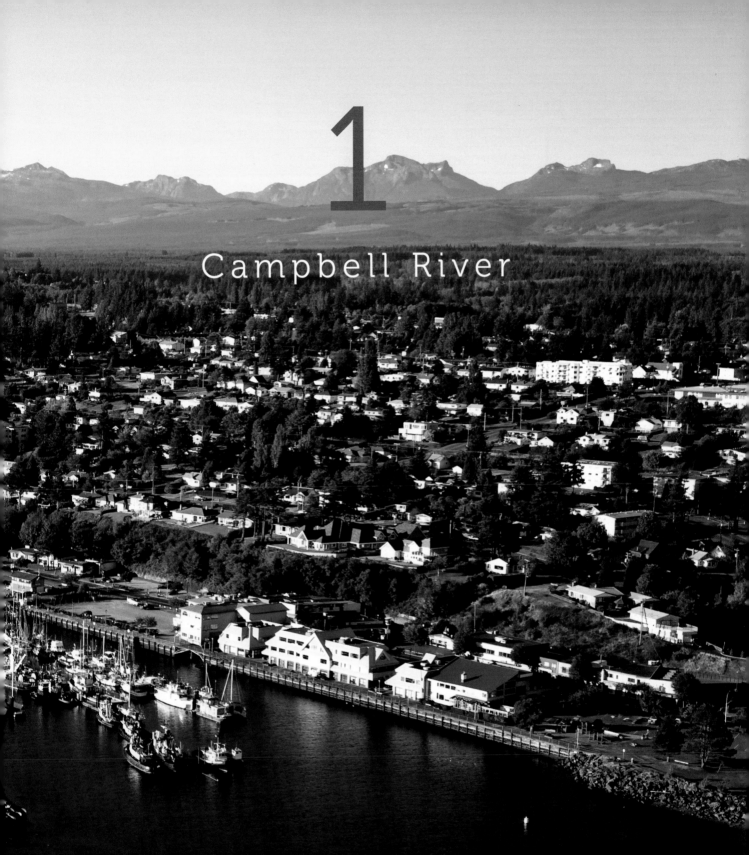

1

Campbell River

Previous pages: Campbell River's
Discovery Pier, fishing harbour,
Maritime Centre and seawalk
anchor the downtown area.

Below: Late afternoon sunlight
highlights patrons at the Salmon
Point Pub located just south of
Campbell River.

Bottom: Participants welcome in
the New Year at the annual Polar
Bear Swim at Saratoga Beach.

Oyster River

The Oyster River starts high up in the mountain backbone of Vancouver Island and flows into the ocean by the resort community of Saratoga Beach, south of Campbell River. Peter Chettleburgh, a Vancouver Island magazine publisher, grew up at a fishing resort that his parents ran on the banks of the Oyster River after World War II.

He remembers barefoot adventures, chasing crabs and fishing for coho salmon in the salt chuck (the local term for saltwater). One of Chettleburgh's neighbours was Barrett Montfort, a wealthy New York investment banker. Montfort liked to troll for salmon but had an aversion to outboard motors. Chettleburgh remembers his father towing Montfort's dinghy on a long line. When Montfort had a fish on, Chettleburgh's dad pulled up the dinghy and helped his client land the fish.

Saratoga Beach, which now has a number of resorts and campgrounds where people can camp and fish, kick-starts the season with a Polar Bear Swim on New Year's Day. Hardy locals don crazy costumes and a bagpiper heralds the first swim. Fisherman's Lodge Pub, upstream from Saratoga Beach by the old Oyster River bridge, has been in operation since the early 1920s. Steelhead trout fishermen, still in their waders, can be found on the outside patio quenching their thirst on a spring afternoon. The pub backs onto the 5-hectare (12-acre) Oyster River Nature Park and many visitors hike pub to pub, following the trail downriver and 2 kilometres (1.2 miles) along the shore to the Salmon Point Resort.

Shelter Point Distillery, a boutique distillery that is a few kilometres north of the Oyster River, is making single malt whisky from locally grown barley. A farmer, local businessman and journalist-turned-whisky-maker have used local wood and stone from Vancouver Island to house the copper stills and condensers constructed in Scotland. Visitors can sample products as they learn about the whisky making process.

Clouds are mirrored in the Oyster River estuary during a low tide.

Caring for Salmon

Local volunteers are helping to restore runs of salmon to the Oyster River by operating a hatchery and constructing side channels, extra river channels that increase the habitat available for small fish. Early one morning in October a crowd, mostly men near retirement, are drinking coffee and getting into waders at the Oyster River Enhancement Society (ORES) hatchery. Today the volunteers will be capturing brood stock, returning adult chinook and coho salmon, which will provide eggs and milt for the hatchery program.

In a pool near the mouth of the river one of the volunteer divers organizes a beach seine net, laying it alongside the pool. Four divers swim the seine ropes across the river. Then the seine net is hauled into the pool and pulled slowly downstream. Volunteers armed with plastic lids bang on the water to scare the fish into the seine.

The seine lines are pulled to shore and the divers maintain a watch to see that the lead line stays on the bottom as the net is shallowed. One female salmon is leaking ripe eggs as she is carried up to the transport tank. The fish are trucked up to the hatchery and kept in a holding pen until the volunteers are ready to create another generation of Oyster River salmon.

Every fall volunteers from the Oyster River Enhancement Society catch returning salmon to provide eggs for their hatchery program.
Ian Douglas photo

Stump Ranchers

The old Island Highway runs the 35 kilometres (21 miles) from Oyster River to Campbell River along a low coastal plane where some of the area's earliest settlers took out quarter-section pre-emptions and clawed small "stump ranches" from the all-enclosing forest. Their hard-won clearings were often reclaimed by the forest after they tired of their efforts and today little remains of these hardy ancients but a few place names such as McGimpsey Road, Stories Beach, Galerno Road and Erickson Road. There are still impressive working fields around the Oyster River where a Gaelic-spouting Nova Scotian named James McIvor carved his cattle ranch from the delta land in 1887, waging his energetic battle against the wilderness well into the twentieth century. Arthur "Bill" Mayse, the beloved local writer who spent much of his long life in the neighbourhood, remembers "The McKeever" as "the definitive oldtimer… with a big barrel chest and craggy features" whose feats of strength were legendary. Once, when a French barque foundered on the Oyster River sandbars and five bodies washed ashore, The McKeever undertook to pack them two at a time up to the "Colonization Road" so the nameless sailors might be taken the 35 kilometres (21 miles) to Comox for a Christian burial. When the government built the Oyster River bridge in 1892, McIvor was reportedly paid double wages because he could lift one end of a bridge timber that required three men on the other end.

Wild Waters

A tugboat towing a self-dumping log barge bucks the current off Cape Mudge.

Just past Oyster River the Island Highway breaks out to the seashore and follows it most of the way into Campbell River, offering a spectacular 30-kilometre (18-mile)

stretch of waterfront driving with unimpeded views across Georgia Strait to the blue mountains of the mainland. The green shores of the Discovery Islands unfold to the north, with lonely Mitlenatch Island, a 36-hectare (14.5-acre) bird sanctuary, sitting by itself out in the middle of the gulf. On a quiet summer day the stretch of ocean adjacent to the highway looks innocent enough, but veteran skippers know the waters below Cape Mudge as one of the most treacherous places on the entire Inside Passage, with a dismaying list of founderings and drownings to prove it. When the prevailing southeast winds that blow up the long reach of Georgia Strait from the US border 200 kilometres (122 miles) away collide with the heavy current ebbing out of Discovery Pass, the effect is a devil's cauldron of monstrous and confused seas that have spelled the end to dozens of small craft and not a few large ones. In 1894 the 30-metre (100-foot) tug *Estelle*, "one of the staunchest of her tonnage in Pacific waters," disappeared with eight hands between Nanaimo and Campbell River, leaving only two sacks of chop feed and a life ring to wash up on this beach. According to Victoria's *British Colonist*, "The majority of those familiar with the district inclined to the belief that the treacherous tide rip that sets [off] Cape Mudge… was responsible." The Campbell River *Courier* reported an eerily similar disaster half a century later when "strong southeast wind and heavy seas off Cape Mudge caused the veteran Vancouver tug S.S. *Petrel* to sink… with all seven hands." It was after a rash of sinkings and strandings by Klondike-bound gold rushers in 1898 that the Cape Mudge Lighthouse was first put into service to help ships find their way safely into Discovery Passage.

A feature that adds immeasurably to the danger of this shore is lack of safe harbours. This was also a great problem to the venerable Iron River Logging Company of

Following pages: The shoreline along Oyster Bay provides Highway 19 travellers with spectacular ocean views.

In the 1930s Oyster Bay was a busy log booming ground protected by a breakwater of old ships.

Sea lions haul out on a rocky
outcropping to sunbathe and
sleep on Mitlenatch Island.

Oyster Bay, which needed a sheltered place to store the logs it harvested and dumped in the water prior to being towed to sawmills. When Al Simpson took over the company in 1930 he was new to the business, but sometimes new eyes can be a good thing for old problems, and Simpson was a can-do sort of guy. It occurred to him that a quick and affordable way to create a breakwater would be to acquire some old decommissioned ships and anchor them off the beach. In the end he assembled a group of fifteen ships, including a World War I destroyer *The President Burns,* and the *St. Paul*, a four-masted sailing ship, all of which became a notable landmark along this otherwise featureless shoreline. The hulks gradually disintegrated in winter southeasters but the area behind the breakwater silted up, providing excellent winter habitat for shorebirds. Dunlin and black-bellied plover feed on the mudflats while black turnstones search the rocky areas around the breakwater for small crustaceans and other food. In time the hulks themselves became an attraction for underwater archaeology buffs, as documented by archaeologist Rick James in *Western Mariner.* Local residents formed a park association in 1989 to protect the shoreline from being developed into a private marina.

Mitlenatch Island

Ten kilometres (6 miles) off the mouth of the Oyster River lies 36-hectare (90-acre) Mitlenatch Island, nicknamed the "Galapagos of the Strait of Georgia" because of the many seabirds nesting on its rocky shores. Pelagic cormorants, double-crested cormorants, pigeon guillemots, black oystercatchers and rhinoceros auklets nest along the shoreline, while walking trails lead visitors to bird blinds where they can observe more than three thousand pairs of glaucous-winged gulls.

Another similarity shared with the Galapagos is Mitlenatch's low rainfall, less than half that of Campbell River, which is only 19 kilometres (12 miles) to the north. This hot, dry environment has resulted in the park being home to many sun-loving plants

Left: Colonies of double-crested cormorants (*Phalacrocorax auritus*) can be viewed preening and nesting on the rocky headlands of the southern tip of Mitlenatch Island in the Strait of Georgia.

Above: Volunteer wardens live in this rustic dwelling on Mitlenatch Island for a week at a time in the summer to ensure visitors do not bring dogs ashore or stray off the paths.

normally associated with a desert climate, such as prickly pear cactus. The island also has some of British Columbia's largest garter snakes, which can often be seen feeding on small fish in the tide pools.

Joy Inglis, an anthropologist living on Quadra Island, has written about First Nations food gathering on Mitlenatch. In the spring immature coho salmon would be caught in stone fish traps and the flowers of the camas plant, the equivalent of a First Nations potato, would be marked with cedar fibre. There are two common camas varieties; bulbs with blue flowers are edible while bulbs with white flowers are poisonous so food gatherers would tag the blue camas stalks. In the fall the marked bulbs would be dug and pit-roasted under a layer of sword fern, salal or skunk cabbage. Other island food plants gathered include wild carrot and beach peas, Indian crabapple, wild onion, fireweed sticks, thistle and bracken fern roots.

Mitlenatch's similarity to the Shetland Islands brought about the next chapter in its history. John Manson and his wife Margaret emigrated from the Shetlands and in 1897 lived on Mitlenatch for a year with their young son to establish a farm. Manson used to row sheep, two at a time, from Cortes Island, which is 7 kilometres (4 miles) away, in a 2.4-metre (8-foot) skiff carved from a cedar log. Cattle were dropped off at the island by a steam tug. The nearest market for his butchered beef or mutton was a 30-kilometre (18-mile) row halfway across the Strait of Georgia to the Vancouver Island settlement of Comox.

Manson was also logging up the coast, so he would row off for weeks at a time, leaving his wife and toddler son to tend the cattle and sheep. Manson took the last sheep off the island in the 1940s. After World War II, the federal government tried to buy the island for a military bombing range. Etta Byers, a Quadra resident and granddaughter of Mike Manson, John's older brother, remembers writing nasty letters to Ottawa opposing this. After her "Uncle John" passed away in 1957, the province bought Mitlenatch and established the island as a provincial park in 1961.

Stories Beach and Shelter Point

Stories Beach is a small clump of homes that harks back to a Scots pioneer named Joseph Stewart, who established a cattle ranch here in 1885 that was taken over in 1909 by his stepson, William Storie. The ranch offered welcome respite to early voyagers. As one wrote in the Comox *Weekly News*, "This is one of the 'out of the world places,' a ranch on the seashore with peace and plenty reigning all around..." By the end of the century all that remained, besides the Stories name, was the crumbling ruin of their fine ranch house beside the highway. A few kilometres farther on, the community of Shelter Point dates back to another pioneer rancher, James Knight, who grew tired of rescuing his pigs from bears and cougars in 1904 and placed this ad in the paper: "I will sell cheap, for cash, my farm of 160 acres, 30 cleared and fenced, together with 45 head of cattle..." There were no takers and the place passed on to his stepson, Sam McGimpsey.

The stump of a forest giant is surrounded by second-growth stands.

The Inland Route

A modern-day traveller who wearies of what is arguably the longest stretch of open seafront driving on any major BC highway has the option of turning inland just south of Ocean Grove and taking the Jubilee Parkway to the Inland Island Highway, which will shave a few minutes off the trip to downtown Campbell River. Most would say this 110-km/h freeway through vacant countryside has little to offer in the way of scenery, but it does provide a glimpse of the kind of terrain that supported some of the world's largest-scale logging operations, the ones that built the city of Campbell River and powered the provincial economy over the past century. Some of the heaviest timber on the planet grew here in the Quinsam River watershed, though the only signs today are giant stumps crumbling amid the new growth. The whole region is still being intensively logged as part of BC's "working forest" and those with an eye for it will be able to identify all stages of the modern harvesting process from recent clearcuts to juvenile plantations to mature regrowth, though the industry's definition of "mature" is shrinking all the time. Photos of the old ERT logging trains seldom show logs smaller than four feet on the butt, while it is rare to see one that large on present-day logging trucks, which tend to be stacked with whippy beanpoles best measured in inches.

If you turn off on Homathko Drive just before the highway, you will end up at Homalco Indian Reserve Number 9. Unlike most First Nations, who have been occupying their reserve lands since time immemorial, the Homalco have only been on this site since the 1980s. A Coast Salish people more closely related to the Klahoose of Cortes Island than the We Wai Kai of Campbell River, they originally occupied the very isolated village of Church House on their traditional lands at the mouth of Bute Inlet but relocated to this new reserve in the 1980s to be nearer to modern amenities. As of the 2006 census, the Homalco had 68 homes on this newly minted reserve and numbered 220 members.

If you follow the parkway across the Inland Highway, you very quickly arrive at the Campbell River Airport. This bustling facility was opened in 1959 after the 1.4 km (4,500 foot) dirt runway was cleared by logging operator Dave Crawford with his bulldozer, assisted by a volunteer team of boy scouts, businessmen, housewives and striking IWA loggers. Soon weekly flights were being offered to Vancouver and during the late 1980s it was not uncommon for the airport to be crowded with corporate jets in the salmon fishing season. Actor Julie Andrews regularly flew up with friends in her pink jet. In 2009 Campbell River Mayor Charlie Cornfield estimated that the airport supported 320 full-time positions and generated $48 million in economic spin-off through aviation-related activities. When federal and provincial funding for a runway extension was announced, opening the airport to Boeing 737 service, the local paper carried a photo of Mayor Cornfield dancing a jig.

Ocean Grove and Willow Point

Back on the coastal route, travellers are often surprised when they stop in Willow Point at the roadside monument to the 50th Parallel and realize that all this travel through all this countryside has only gotten them one degree into Canada, which goes on for another 32. The neighbourhood of Willow Point bills itself as "The Gateway to Campbell River" and marks the edge of urban sprawl that increases in density all the way into the city centre. Originally a cluster of small ranches with a store and gas station, the Willow Point Community Hall was added in 1940 and remains a favourite venue for dinner theatre productions to this day. Willow Point joined the Campbell River municipality in 1969 and has grown into one of the more sought-after places to live with easy access to medical offices, restaurants, retail stores, pub and the popular Ken Forde Beach, named after the straight-talking Willow Point gas station operator who became mayor of Campbell River.

The 50th Parallel marker alongside Campbell River's shoreline is rarely snow-covered for any length of time in the maritime climate.

Taking in the view near Willow Point from a vintage convertible car brings back a lot of fun memories.

Above: Ken Forde Park displays an anchor from the wreck of the *Thomas Woodward*, which went down off Willow Point in 1868.

Top right: Glaciers deposited the Big Rock on the foreshore, where it has become a Campbell River icon.

Right: The waterfront seawalk, extending 6 km north from Willow Point to First Avenue, is a hit with visitors and locals.

Four Square Miles

As it enters the old Campbell River townsite, which is the current downtown, the highway dips down what was once a murderous hill famous for runaway jalopies and enters onto the low plain of the Campbell River core. Roughly two miles square with the river running along its northern edge and the seashore along the east, the city layout still reflects the aspirations and enmities of its earliest occupants.

Originally, of course, it was held by a branch of the K'omoks Salish, who were displaced by the Laichwiltach in one of the significant exchanges of First Nations territory that occurred in BC after European contact. Both of these groups favoured the land around the river mouth for their village sites, especially on the commodious spit that juts up from the south, creating a placid basin ideal for beaching dugout canoes. When non-Native settlers first began arriving, they were granted pre-emptions in quarter sections (160 acres/65 hectares) and several of these were granted in the 1880s to John Barton Hills and the Nunns brothers, the Nunnses choosing riverbank land upstream from the Wei Wai Kum settlement.

Hills planted his claim stakes at the opposite corner of the Campbell River lowland from the Nunnses, taking up waterfront acreage that overlaps the coastal sector of the modern downtown, though the shoreline has migrated eastward since his time. He built a rough shack at what would today be the north corner of Tenth Avenue and proceeded to establish a bit of a neighbourhood party house according to the disapproving Fred Nunns, probably augmenting his other subsistence activities by indulging in the fine old coast tradition of bootlegging. Nunns greeted the news that Hills was thinking of selling out by scratching in his diary, "I hope he does, as he is not a very

Left: The bright red torii gate in Sequoia Park overlooking Discovery Passage was donated by Ishikari, Campbell River's twin city in Japan.

Above: Dick Murphy Park is a popular place to walk and watch the rowboats fishing just offshore in the Tyee Pool.

good neighbour." Hills was the only other white settler in the area, but that was one too many for finicky Fred. In 1892 Hills did sell out to a family named Peacey, who made two noteworthy contributions during their short stay. First, they produced John Campbell Peacey, the first non-Native person to claim Campbell River as his place of birth. Second, when they decided there had to be something better to do with their lives than wrestling with tough Vancouver Island stumps, they sold their 160-acre (65-hectare) property with its hard-won 7 acres (3 hectares) of cleared fields to the people who would put Campbell River on the map—the brothers Thulin.

It is a matter of record that Campbell River was not the Thulins' first, or even second, choice of location for their gateway city. Charlie Thulin, later revered as the founding father of Campbell River, at first scoffed at the site as a "useless spot in which to settle" and in 1889 he and his younger brother Fred made their stand at Lund on the mainland side, where there was a natural harbour. After watching events unfold over the next five years, however, the Thulins revised their opinion and decided to implement a two-pronged strategy by setting up on both sides of the strait. Not only was the Vancouver Island side attracting the heaviest logging activity, with over three hundred men working in the surrounding forest and more arriving every day, there was a surprisingly brisk traffic in recreational fishing targeting the jumbo spring salmon that schooled at the mouth of the Campbell. The Thulin brothers began looking for property and had chosen a site at Willow Point when they ran into a logger named Joe Thompson who had put together a deal to buy the Peacey place for the bargain price of $800 but couldn't complete because he'd blown his stake in the bright lights of Comox. The brothers paid over the $800 (some say $600) in his stead and that, according to Thompson's descendents, is why Campbell River owes its existence to the fleshpots of Comox.

The Thulins wasted no time putting plans for their second marine gateway into action. In Charlie's words, "On March 11, 1904, we went from Lund to Campbell River across the Strait with a load of timber, a wagon and a horse loaded on the barge. At that time there was not a single white man in that place for miles around. By the first of July we had built a hotel and had it ready for business." This first of three Willows hotels was a modest affair of thirteen rooms located near the present site of the Tidemark Theatre between Eleventh and Thirteenth avenues on Shoppers Row (it really was at the high tide mark then, before the shallow beach fronting it was filled in to create the Tyee Plaza in 1959). The hotel was a hit from the get-go, taking up where Hills's party shack had left off in providing for the R-and-R needs of coastal loggers, a function it would dutifully carry on for half a century. As a logger named Dahlby remembered, "The men came from all around to drink at the saloon, pulling their boats up on the beach. There were card games and a drink of whisky cost 10 cents. Most of the men slept outside in blankets." While the loggers' demand for cheap whisky could be depended on year-round, it was not what you could call value-added business. That was provided by the gentleman anglers, who came for long stays and wanted the best in dining, accommodation and general pampering. Catering to two such dissimilar clienteles was a constant challenge. Within a year the Thulins removed the bar to a separate building called the Logger's Annex, 50 yards (45 metres) away, but it wasn't far enough. As a sportsman by the name of Sir John Rogers griped in 1908, "till the small hours of the morning the sound of revelry from the bar was not conducive to a good night's rest." Many sporty types preferred to stay in the rustic tents out on the spit provided by Ned and June Painter and when the Painters built their eponymous lodge in 1940 the Willows lost the high-end part of the fishing trade for good. By that time the logging industry was going so strong it hardly mattered.

In 1909 the brothers built a second hotel, but it burnt down within a few months, cremating the company bookkeeper. Undaunted, they set to work on a third and grander Willows kitty-corner from the present Discovery Inn, an eighty-room edifice with plenty of space to keep the timber beasts and anglers apart—they hoped. The scale and elegance of this building took more than one city visitor by surprise, as the chronicler of the Price Ellison Expedition reported while passing through on the survey that led to the creation of Strathcona Park in 1910. "The Captain had told us there was a good hotel but we had no reason to believe it would be as good as this," gushed H. McLure Johnson. Rooms featured brass beds, hot and cold running water and the

saloon had a spectacular bar consisting of a solid slab of Douglas fir 60 feet long and 3 feet wide (18 by 1 metre), with tiled floor, mirrors and ornamental iron ceiling. The elegant touches, including the ambitious dining room menu, were a credit to Charlie Thulin's wife, Mary, who took care of business while the men were busy running their logging operation and adding to their empire. The Campbell River Museum has a recreation of the interior of the Willows and examples of the early salmon fishing gear used by sportsmen.

In 1904 the Thulins opened the Willows Hotel (at left) and the "Logger's Annex," which stood where Campbell River's Tidemark Theatre is located today.
Helen Mitchell Collection, Museum of Campbell River 8248

The perennial "logger problem" was dealt with, Johnson wrote, by restricting the tame apes "to one end of the hotel and the corridors leading to their rooms are separated from the rest of the hotel by partitions and closed doors so that the loggers, if inclined to be boisterous, will not interfere with the patrons of the hotel of quieter instincts." As before, this containment strategy owed more to hope than reality, especially when the timber beasts got their blood up.

One thing that got their blood up in the fall of 1917 was the news that something called Prohibition was about to outlaw their favourite pastime, and they descended on the hotel determined, as historian Helen Mitchell wrote, to "make the most of their last night of legalized drinking... There were no glasses or bottles washed that night. As they were emptied, the loggers smashed them down upon the tiled floor and soon everybody was wading and sliding around in a welter of broken glass. Then they started throwing bottles at each other..." Charlie Thulin's son Carl was helping at the bar and later maintained that the only thing that saved the hotel from utter destruction was that the bush apes all started fighting and shifted outside so as to have room to do it properly. When they had dealt with whatever metaphysical disagreement it was to everyone's satisfaction and tried to return to the task of drinking up the hotel's whisky, they found the staff had spiked the doors shut.

The Quinsam Hotel, for years the destination of choice for loggers and fishermen, remains popular with locals looking for a lively night out.

The Ideal Café, a landmark restaurant in Campbellton, is known for its home-cooked meals.

Using the resources of their first town to finance and provision their second, the Thulins sponsored the building of a steamship-capable wharf, a school, a hospital and a dance pavilion in Campbell River. They also added to their own enterprises with a store, several homes, apartments, a logging company, a sawmill, several tugboats and a dairy farm. As trade increased the brothers replaced their original buildings with larger ones, complementing their landmark hotel with a new two-storey department store located at the head of the wharf where the green-roofed Georgia Quay complex stands today.

One thing they didn't do, however, was let anybody else get a foothold on their turf. All the private businesses and all the available land was held in the steely grip of the brothers themselves. The settlement was referred to, not always kindly, as "Thulin-ville," and it had some of the exclusionary aspects of a company town. In the end this may have contributed to the downfall of the Thulin empire. Independent businesses and settlers were forced to look outside city limits for land. The Wei Wai Kum were not selling any of their land, so the only significant landholder left to deal with was old Fred Nunns on his riverbank block upstream from the reserve. Nunns was open to the occasional sale when the mood struck him, and at one point relinquished an 80-acre (32-hectare) block, near the present highway bridges, to Klondike Smith, who in 1922 surveyed it into building lots, creating the valley's first modern subdivision. So a rival townsite called Campbellton began to spring up at the opposite corner of the Campbell River lowland from Thulinville. Centred on the redoubtable Quinsam Hotel, Campbellton remains a distinct neighbourhood to this day. In equal parts due to the new competition, the post-World War I recession and a habit of extending credit to anyone who asked for it, the Thulins went into receivership in 1923 and ended up losing everything but their home, their farm and some of their land. Hard as this was for

Above: Colourful murals dot the downtown area around the fishing harbour.

Left: The Pier Street Market, held weekly at the Maritime Heritage Centre parking lot, attracts locals and visitors alike for the handmade crafts and fresh food products from the Campbell River area.

the Thulins, it brought in a new set of entrepreneurs with fresh energy and new ideas that opened up Campbell River.

A Waterfront Town

Those approaching Campbell River via the old Island Highway rather than the new freeway get to see the town put its best foot forward. It began as a waterfront town and the most interesting features are still along the busy, much-modernized water-front. This is in large part due to the vision of councils led by Mayor Bob Ostler in the 1980s, which set out to reorient the town to its most vital feature and make sure it didn't fall victim to the inland creep that beset Nanaimo and other coastal towns. The plan succeeded perhaps beyond anything its framers intended, as the town's main assets—the transportation arteries, prime shopping area, top cultural and hospitality facilities, sights and, until recently, main employment generator, are all strung along the waterfront.

The downtown section of the highway has been renamed with a welcome sign that declares it to be the "Soul of Campbell River." Marine-themed restaurants and stores like Crabby Bob's Seafood were encouraged. The old sewage plant, a despised blight upon the downtown left over from the no-frills Bob Forde era, was deodorized and reincarnated as the Maritime Heritage Centre, a museum showcasing Campbell River's marine history. It houses Campbell River's most celebrated boat along with a display of more than seven hundred marine artefacts such as whaling harpoons and vintage radio sets collected by Robert Somerville, a retired Campbell River oph-thalmologist. The conference room is the venue for the popular Words on the Water Writers' Festival that has brought in authors and poets for workshops and readings every spring since 2002.

Hard by the Maritime Heritage Centre is the heart of Campbell River's working waterfront, the government wharf. Construction of the first breakwater and commercial harbour in 1950 was a great event for the small village, allowing it to fulfill its destiny as seaport to the Discovery Coast. Before then, the winter storms had made it a place to avoid in a small boat and even steamships steered clear of it in bad weather. After the coming of protected year-round moorage, its nearness to the major fishing grounds in Johnstone Strait made it a natural home for the salmon fleet and many fishermen built homes in the area.

Previous pages: There is a waiting list in the Discovery Harbour Marina for moorage of recreational boats as more and more people retire in the area.

The government wharf is a good place to spend a few hours strolling if you want to soak up the maritime flavours that have defined Campbell River over the years. On one weekday morning a shellfish farmer is unloading sacks of oysters, the steady whine of a hydraulic crane punctuated by the cries of crows and gulls. The crows are scavenging the briny creatures that encrust the oyster sacks while the gulls are dropping clam shells onto the dock, using gravity to crack them open. Small speedboats, maritime mini-vans used to access the outer islands, are rafted to aluminum work skiffs. A converted gillnetter, modified to drag the bottom of the ocean for swimming scallops, is tied up in front of a loading barge being re-powered. A logger hustles down the dock ramp with a pair of worn caulk boots and spare engine parts, lugs down a bucket of oil and then roars off to park his pickup. A few minutes later his battered aluminum crew boat burbles into the loading area and he grabs his gear to head out to his logging show on a nearby island.

In the space of a morning you can watch a capsule history of this area unfold before your eyes. The large fleet of commercial fishboats that once had this dock area humming with activity—pint-sized gillnetters, medium-sized trollers with their antenna-

Twilight settles in on the working vessels in the fishing harbour.

like poles and a famous fleet of big, heroic-looking seiners—has been hard hit by the decline in fish stocks, leaving many once-proud seine boats with *For Sale* signs in their portholes and barnacles on their bottoms. For decades these husky vessels represented the aristocracy of the BC fishing fleet. A man who skippered or owned a seiner was a man to be reckoned with, and many Laichwiltach acquired seiners—some had several—representing a high-water mark in First Nations adaptation and achievement.

It is indicative of the current state of affairs that the most prominent seine boat in Campbell River these days is a museum exhibit. Any Canadian over the age of 20 would recognize the *BCP 45* in a flash, though they may not know it by its nondescript name. Indeed, it is the only west coast boat that could give the east coast cod schooner *Bluenose* a run for the title of most recognizable fishboat in the country, and for the same reason—it was on our money. The *BCP 45* is a classic 1927 table seiner that spent six decades working the tides, mostly out of Campbell River with a Laichwiltach crew. In 1958 vacationing Ontario photographer George Hunter happened to snap her picture pulling in a sockeye set in a group of seiners near Ripple Point, just north of town and the image found its way onto the Canadian five-dollar bill issued in 1972 and circulated until 1986. The skipper at the time the photo was taken was the late Mel Assu with crew members Andy Dick, Fred Seville, Ron Forrest, Allen Chickite and Allen Mearns. Chickite later owned the boat and displayed it at Expo 86 in Vancouver, where it was rated the sixth best out of 185 exhibits. After stripping its licence in 1998 he donated the floating icon to the Vancouver Maritime Museum, but they didn't know what to do with it and in 2002 the old gal was tucked into the new Maritime Heritage Centre back in its home port where it was lovingly restored by a crew of volunteers led by local boat builder Buford Haines. On September 19, 2005, the *BCP 45* was officially declared a national historic site.

Salmon Farming

Today if you see a boat hauling fish or gear around the Campbell River waterfront, likely as not it's connected to the salmon farming industry, which has three major corporations headquartered in town along with many companies supplying such services as fish processing, nets and maintenance, transportation, packaging, containers, diving services, machinery and equipment. With the pulp mill shut down, the aquaculture industry has become the largest employer in the area, with two land-based hatcheries, several processing companies and twenty grow-out sites.

Fish farming got started in BC in the 1980s using native species but switched to faster-growing Atlantic salmon under the influence of Norwegian investors, who had pioneered the industry in Europe and were eager to expand into Canada. The once-shaky BC industry has now stabilized under the domination of three large Norwegian-owned corporations that have pretty much perfected the process.

Hatcheries typically take eggs from disease-screened brood stock in the fall and raise them in fresh water for 12 to 18 months until they are ready to go to saltwater. Before delivery the fish are sorted and vaccinated against common viruses then are transported by trucks and boats to the net pen grow-out sites. Here the fish are raised for 18 to 24 months until they reach a size of 5.5 kilograms (12 pounds), when they are harvested. The fish are fed by computer-controlled feeders and monitored with underwater cameras.

Top: A welder and ship-painter relax during a break while refitting a tugboat at the Ocean Pacific shipyard.

Bottom: The *BCP 45*, famous for once gracing the back of the five-dollar bill, lies in state at the Maritime Heritage Museum.

The open net-cage fish farming industry in BC coastal waters has proponents on both sides fighting for their particular opinions. This farm is near Toba Inlet.

Salmon farming has been controversial in BC, mostly because of its impact on wild stocks and on traditional salmon fishing. Opponents like biologist Alexandra Morton claim open net pens nurture plagues of sea lice that attack wild salmon at the juvenile stage and threaten native stocks with exotic diseases, among other things. There is tension between the new kids on the docks and the old guard. Out-of-work seine boat crewmen eye busy fish farmers with the hostile glare of cowmen squaring off with farmers in the Old West. Where it will end nobody knows.

Round the Island Yacht Race

Campbell River also has a large population of pleasure boats, and with its excellent facilities is becoming an ever more popular stop for the adventurous yachter. The first organized yacht race around Vancouver Island was developed in 1986 by local multihull sailors Wayne Gorrie and Steve Knight. Although 25 boats signed up for the initial event, the starting gun was never fired because of sponsorship snags.

Eleven years later the Van Isle 360° International Yacht Race was born. The first year, 14 boats raced around the island over a period of two weeks, with ten stops along the way, including Campbell River. The finish line for Campbell River is just off the 50th Parallel marker in order to avoid the extreme currents farther north in Discovery Passage.

In recent years, television and movie crews follow the entire race and the Van Isle 360° has grown into one of the most respected and exciting yacht races on the entire west coast of North America.

Opposite page: Racing and cruising yachts are drawn to the waters around the Discovery Islands and the world-famous coves of Desolation Sound.

Discovery Fishing Pier

The Discovery Pier is an elevated sportfishing platform that runs along the outside of the government breakwater next to the fishboat docks, resembling the old government wharf of the steamship era, which was in the same general area. It was built by the City in 1987 as the centrepiece of the waterfront revitalization program, aimed

at playing up Campbell River's image as "Salmon Capital of the World." It must be said that its original purpose has been somewhat blunted by the decline in salmon fishing but, nonetheless, it has become a great people place and focal point of the waterfront. It is perhaps more popular for strolling, sightseeing and community events such as the farmers' market and the Huck Fin Fishing Derby for kids than its builders foresaw but it is a rare day when there aren't at least a few serious anglers out on the pier trying their luck. The main targets of veteran pier fishermen are chinook salmon in July and August when the smaller pink salmon are also present. Coho show up in September through to November and a few hardy souls fish for winter chinook off the pier in January and February. The largest fish so far caught from the pier is a 50-pound (23-kilogram) chinook. Because the pier is so high off the water, the tricky part is getting the hooked fish into a net, which must be dropped down on a rope.

Robert V. Ostler Foreshore Park

Robert V. Ostler Foreshore Park, between the public marina and Tyee Plaza, commemorates the 1980s Campbell River mayor who made renewal of the downtown waterfront his personal cause. The park is perfect for kite flying and hosts many celebrations such as the annual Salmon Festival held on Canada Day. On Canada Day 1972 the Heritage Pavilion, a First Nation-style "big house," was opened in the park. Local First Nation carvers Sam Henderson and his sons, Ernie and Bill, along with Bob Neel, Ben Dick, Eugene Alfred and Dora Cook carved the massive beams and poles.

Canada Day Parade

Canada Day is Campbell River's big day. The first settlers of the Discovery Coast began making a practice of gathering on the spit for July First celebrations dating back to about 1898 and the Thulin brothers picked up on this theme by planning the building of their historic first Willows Hotel so it could be opened amid great fanfare on July 1, 1904. The second and third incarnations of the Willows were also opened on successive July Firsts in 1909 and 1910, each time with hundreds of guests, tons of food and barrels of free whisky. Ever since, the First of July has been Campbell River's main occasion for exercising community spirit.

In perfect weather, sunny with a cooling breeze off the water, the 2009 Canada Day parade wound through downtown. People set lawn chairs up along the route and Robert Ostler Park was festive with activities from bouncy castles to a concert stage.

Former mayor Lynn Nash, representing CR Seniors, was driving a beautifully restored

Top: The Discovery Pier and the fishing harbour breakwater are familiar landmarks on the Campbell River waterfront.

Bottom: Ice cream melts faster than these two little girls can keep up with on a warm summer day at Discovery Pier.

Opposite page: Canada Day celebrations include a fireworks display that can be enjoyed from Rebecca Spit on Quadra Island.

antique automobile. Many floats featured water guns and sprinklers to cool down the crowd, which included a large St. Bernard. A monster truck from Saratoga Speedway caused a ripple of excitement in the younger members watching. After a First Nations Welcome Song there was a rousing version of "O Canada" and cake for everyone. People listened to the music and picnicked on blankets under the trees, toddlers tumbling around them. As the evening light dimmed, more and more spectators moved to the water's edge. There were spectators on top of Tyee Plaza, and many people parked beside the Discovery Harbour Marina and set up chairs in the back of their pickups.

The Coast Guard cutter *Point Race* made sure that there was a safe distance between the firework barge and the more than thirty yachts anchored out in the Passage. The view from the top deck of the Quadra ferry was spectacular with the navigation lights of the watching vessels twinkling in between showers of cascading stars.

The Coast Guard

Close by the Quadra ferry dock just north of Robert Ostler Park is the base for the 21-metre (70-foot) Coast Guard Cutter *Point Race*. Captain Geoff Saunders, a soft-spoken 35-year Coast Guard veteran with a brown beard touched with salt and pepper, has patrolled Campbell River waters for 19 years. Capt. Saunders has seen many changes in the last two decades patrolling Discovery Passage. On the negative side the commercial salmon fishing season has been cut way back. On the positive side search and rescue calls are down about 15 percent due to the more reliable engines on recreational boats.

Saunders remembers one memorable rescue when a tugboat skipper fell overboard off Quadra Island in March 2009. Ocean water temperatures are so cold that

Almost a million passengers travel through Discovery Passage on cruise ships each year.

A Cormorant search and rescue helicopter hovers over a rescue boat for a mid-air transfer training mission near CFB Comox.

a ten-minute immersion can be fatal. When the tug sent out a distress call the *Point Race* fired up her engines and started a search. The captain and crew of the Campbell River-based seiner *Pacific Faith* found the victim, after he had been drifting in the frigid waters for more than an hour. He was quickly transferred to the *Point Race,* where rescue specialists were able to start treating him for hypothermia by bringing his body temperature up slowly with warmed oxygen.

Approximately a million cruise passengers go past Campbell River and through Discovery Passage each year on their way to and from Alaska. Huge barges carry freight from Seattle north to small communities. Tugs towing massive self-dumping log barges regularly make the trip past Campbell River. Most pass without incident, but Paul Nestman, a rescue specialist serving on the *Point Race*, remembers the summer night in 1984 when the cruise ship *Sundancer* hit the Quadra shoreline just north of Campbell River and started taking on water. The ship limped to the nearby mill dock and then sank alongside, collapsing the dock. Thanks to the Coast Guard and local search and rescue all 787 passengers and crew were safely evacuated.

Logger Mike and the Tyee Plaza

Moving north from the government marina the shoreline until 1959 looped inland to form a shallow bight called Willow Bay. In a highly controversial move, a local developer won provincial backing to fill in the bay, creating 14 acres (5.6 hectares) of new land with an attached marina. Today this is the site of the Tyee Plaza Shopping Centre and the Quadra Island ferry terminal with the Discovery Inn and Robert Ostler Park at its south end, plus the downtown's most generous parking lot, and it would be hard to imagine the city without it. The plaza's most intriguing feature is Logger Mike, a larger-than-life carving of a man climbing a six-storey wooden pole, Campbell River's tribute to the forest industry that moulded the character of the town even more than the fishing industry.

Logger Mike was carved by Dean Lemke in 1983. Each Christmas he sports a Santa suit.

Mike vies with the Big Rock, Discovery Pier, Elk Falls and *BCP 45* as Campbell River's most photographed emblem and is a folksy representation of the glamour job in the old-time woods, a high rigger topping a spar tree. In the days of high-lead logging, before the arrival of steel spars, grapple yarders, hoe-chuckers and helicopters, crews threaded their lines through blocks hung in tall trees so that logs could be hoisted above entanglements on the ground as they were being yarded into the landing area to be loaded onto rail cars or trucks for transport to tidewater. The job of the high rigger was to climb a suitably large Douglas fir (yellow cedars like Mike's peeled and varnished showpiece were not big enough or strong enough) and trim off the limbs and top, then strap on a mess of rigging so complex a tall ship would seem simplistic by comparison. It was dangerous work requiring athleticism and a cool head, and every young whistle punk or chokerman dreamed of becoming a high rigger, though there were jobs in camp that had more responsibility and better pay. Mike is an old-time high rigger who used an axe rather than a chainsaw for his tree-trimming, as can be seen by the authentically short-handled rigger's axe dangling beneath him. He appears to have finished topping this little pecker-pole and may be going back down to pick up the straw line so that he can start pulling up the guy lines that will prevent the spar from toppling when the steam yarder begins pulling in turns of big six-foot-thick peelers. At Christmastime Mike sometimes dons a Santa suit, which is in character. Riggers were notorious show-offs.

Right: Bird's-eye view of an operator in his wood processor, hoisting and cutting second-growth fir to length.

Below: Sparks from a train ignited a pile of logs in the summer of 1938, creating the Great Bloedel Fire, seen here from the Campbell River estuary. Museum of Campbell River 16835

Bottom: A contractor working with Western Forest Products is about to set out with a load of hemlock logs harvested from a cutblock north of Campbell River.

Logging on the Coast

In the late 1860s logging started on Quadra and Read islands, where the timber could be easily taken from the shoreline by solitary handloggers who felled the trees into the water and towed them to sawmills. As logging operations grew in the 1880s, large camps using oxen, horses, steam donkeys—such as the one exhibited behind the museum—and later trains to transport logs were set up in the vicinity of Campbell River. Logging became the backbone of the Campbell River economy with rail lines running right through the small settlement to log-dumps in the river estuary. Nearby Menzies Bay was home to some of the largest logging camps in the world and smaller operations dotted every bay and island on the Discovery Coast, all looking to Campbell River as their nearest source of groceries, parts, booze and, with any luck, dames. After World War II, trains were replaced by trucks that could run on steeper grades to access timber on the sidehills up from valley bottoms, while chainsaws took over from axes and crosscut saws. Nowadays, in second-growth forests, harvesting timber has become mechanized and computerized with all-in-one processing machines like feller-bunchers, which can cut logs from the stump and trim limbs many times faster than a man with a chainsaw. Logging will continue as long as trees grow and people use wood, but it will never be the job-generator it was. Campbell River celebrates its logging heritage by holding a logger's sports day in Nunns Creek Park.

Planted seedlings growing within a clearcut in the Big Tree area near Sayward are protected with deer-proof covers.

No discussion of Campbell River's logging history is complete without mention of the Great Bloedel Fire. The summer of 1938 was unusual. The bush was tinder dry, and instead of laying off workers during the normal fire season the loggers were still busy on July 5 when sparks from a passing train at the Bloedel, Stewart and Welch camp by Boot Lake, 25 kilometres (15 miles) west of Campbell River, ignited a deck of logs. The fire quickly burned out of control and headed south. For six weeks more than 1,500 men battled the flames. Two destroyers, HMCS *Fraser* and the *Laurent*, were anchored in Duncan Bay in case they were needed to evacuate citizens of Campbell River. Luckily the fire missed the town and afterward there was a massive replanting program to replace the 30,000 hectares (74,000 acres) of trees burned in the fire. The destruction of so much timber brought dire predictions of economic collapse, but somehow the local forest industry kept growing for another fifty years, carrying Campbell River—and the province of BC—on its back. Today many pundits are once again chorusing logging's demise—even arguing that it's time to take Logger Mike down from his pedestal as town mascot—but they overlook the fact that the vast hinterland surrounding town is still 99 percent covered in young trees, all hungrily reaching for the sun. Whether or not the fragile salmon resource can be brought back is very much open to question, and the last Strathcona mine is scheduled to expire in 2012, but as sure as the rains will keep falling, the trees will keep growing and playing some part in the community's future.

Logger Sports

The annual Logger Sports Show is held at Nunns Creek Park behind the Ironwood Mall. Competitors from as far away as Nova Scotia and New Zealand travel to vie for the $32,000 in prize money. Jim Lilburn, head of the Canadian Logger Sports Association, explains that contests like birling or log-rolling are heritage events since most wood is dry-land sorted these days. In the past, logs would be dumped into the water and collected into rafts called booms, and making up booms required good log-walking skills. Tree-climbing abilities like Mike's are no longer needed for rigging wooden spars but have been revived by helicopter logging, where trees are limbed, topped and cut almost through before being plucked away by the chopper. Bucking contests recall the days of steam-powered equipment when felled logs had to be sectioned or bucked into short blocks to make firewood. Axe-throwing and speed-chopping recall the skills of the axemen who split the firewood and did an array of demanding tasks. Anyone wondering if logging is a lost art should watch the amazing 8- to 11-year-olds who compete.

Participants in the annual Logger Sports compete in a series of events such as the Chainsaw Race, Double Buck, Axe Throw and Log Rolling.

In the birling competition the idea is to try to roll the log so your fellow contestant falls off. After the contestants have a practice on the log, they shake hands and then walk the log out to the middle of the pond while holding onto a pike pole for balance. Once the announcer calls out "steady the log, throw your poles, time in," the contest begins. The concentration is intense as each person tries to run the other contestant off the log. Both are watching each other's feet. When Darren Hudson and three-time world champion Wade Stewart face off, the muscles in the back of their legs are straining as they run forwards and backwards, a delicate balancing act that ends with a dunking.

During the tree-climbing event two contestants, rigged with spurs and safety loops, race to the top of the tree, ring the bell and then descend in a barely controlled fall featuring suicidal leaps. There are also contests showcasing skills at lassoing logs with the heavy steel cables known as "chokers" and in the expert operation of very loud chainsaws.

The Campbell River Indian Band and Discovery Harbour Centre

The commercial zone used to peter out north of the Tyee Plaza, and city boosters despaired that some of the downtown's most strategic land was lying fallow in the Campbell River Indian Band's 350-acre (142-hectare) Reserve Number 11. They needn't have worried. In 1998 the band and its development partner unveiled a new shopping/marina/cruise ship complex, which represented such an upgrade on existing facilities that critics fretted the band had gone too far. The new shopping centre brought in big-box retailers that put existing businesses under pressure and, in the minds of some, created an oversupply of retail space. The cruise ship terminal, which was developed in partnership with the City, got off to a slow start and had critics pointing fingers. But the expansive new centre, handsomely decorated with poles and archways carved by the Henderson family, moved the city's centre of balance emphatically back to the waterfront and now stands as a beacon of optimism that goes a considerable way to offset the gloom caused by the decline of resource industries.

The Discovery Harbour Marina is the centre of recreational boating in the area. Built by the Campbell River Band in 1990, millions of tons of rocks were trucked in to form what is by far Campbell River's most extensive breakwater. The marina has berths for 525 vessels from 5 metres (18 feet) to 55 metres (180 feet) in length. The Campbell River Band also runs the fuel station, and amenities such as grocery stores, marine supply stores and restaurants in the nearby Discovery Mall make the marina a popular stopover for yachts heading up the coast.

It had been a long journey for the Laichwiltach. The museum has a 1923 photo of one of the last longhouses to remain standing on the spit, that of the Quatelle family, and it had the proportions of a hockey arena. It is instructive to close one's eyes and imagine the waterfront studded with these enormous structures, smoke lying low over the sea, loaded dugouts the size of gillnetters coming and going, boys whooping, girls screaming, babies crying and figures scurrying over every flat surface as numerous as ants… and not all that long ago. About the time North America and Europe were being joined by the first telegraph cable, the Laichwiltach tribes had a combined population of four to ten thousand and the Campbell River was one of their chief gathering places, a site where many different groups congregated during the bountiful salmon runs. The Laichwiltach were a force in the world and no other coastal peoples dared use the Inside Passage without their consent, but they were about to be defeated by an invisible enemy—the smallpox virus, which decimated their ranks in 1862, taking their wise elders and strong leaders and reducing their numbers to a dispirited handful.

First Nation greeters wait for travellers to disembark at the Wei Wai Kum cruise ship terminal in Campbell River.

The *Hanseatic*, a specialized pocket cruise ship, stops at Campbell River's Wei Wai Kum cruise ship terminal in Discovery Passage.

The Quatelle family's traditional
big house at Campbell River Spit,
Wei Wai Kum Reserve, ca.1923.
Clinton Wood Collection,
Museum of Campbell River 6013

Things got worse for the Laichwiltach before they got better. Through the latter half of the nineteenth century, their numbers continued to be eroded by waves of European diseases and their traditional lands began to be taken up by a growing influx of settlers. Despite their problems, however, the old battling spirit endured and the We Wai Kum tried to meet the new challenges head-on. A Wei Wai Kum chief named Captain John Kwaksistala (of the prominent Campbell River family whose surname was later anglicized to Quocksister) set up permanent domicile on the spit in the 1880s, most of the Wei Wai Kum following him over time. When the Nunns family staked out a large section of the Campbell River flood plain for their ranch, Kwaksistala convinced the government surveyor to repatriate some of the land the Nunnses had begun cultivating, much to crusty Frederick Nunns's chagrin. It would be one of the Wei Wai Kum's only victories in their long land-claim struggle, which continues today. The We Wai Kum cleared land for agriculture, started their own logging operation and entered the commercial fishing industry as they struggled against discriminatory laws and attitudes to hold their own in a rapidly transforming world, but for a long time it seemed a losing battle. As Chief Lul-kaweelis told a Royal Commission in 1914:

Since the white men have come and are still coming more and more they are making our places here smaller all the time and that is what pains our hearts. This place has been measured three times and each time it has been made smaller... We

A thunderbird totem helps to support the massive cedar beams inside the Kwanwatsi Big House.
Ian Douglas photo

ask permission that we be allowed to take the fish out of the river with nets even if it is only a short one. Nearly every winter we come close to starving because we are not allowed to take fish out of the river… The drinking house over here is too close to our reserve… It is a very bad thing. It is just like murdering people…

Over the course of the twentieth century the band clawed its way back. By the time of the 2006 census, total population had risen to 381 from a low of 61 in 1914.

Although only 3 percent of today's Wei Wai Kum speak native Kwakwala at home, they retain strong connections with their past and still honour many of their ancient traditions. Traditional culture centres on the Kwanwatsi Big House, located across from the Discovery Mall, where ceremonies such as potlatches are held. A huge graphic of a two-headed sea serpent, Sisiutl, guards the front entrance. Inside, large totems topped with thunderbirds support a carved crossbeam bearing two massive cedar logs running the length of the big house. A painted screen covers one end of the building where there are benches for drummers and singers. In the middle there is a large sand-covered dance floor with a fire pit in the centre. A row of chairs circles the dance floor and on both sides of the building there are six levels of bench seating.

During a potlatch a family validates their rights to crests and privileges that have been handed down to them. Daisy Sewid, an elder who helps organize ceremonies, explains that "everything we put on the dance floor is a dramatization of our history, because we didn't write. It's oral history, we dramatize when we have our potlatches and that's how we pass it on to our children and that's how you verify your right to these dances." Invited guests are given gifts and by accepting these gifts, they acknowledge that these rights and privileges belong to the family.

A Modern Potlatch

Harold Sewid, with his wife Cindy by his side, hosted his first potlatch as a new clan chief in 2009 in honour of his late father Bob Sewid and his late eldest aunt Dora Sewid-Cook. Blankets on benches reserve places for family members who greet each other with lots of hugs. Bags of

Bags of flour and rice that will be given away during the potlatch are stacked by the entrance poles. Ian Douglas photo

flour and rice that will be given away are stacked by the entrance poles. At the other end of the building a table draped with a traditional button blanket holds a photo of Dora while propped against the table is a large portrait of Bob Sewid. Elders begin to fill the chairs around the dance floor while kids chase each other up and down the benches. Wood smoke slowly curls from the fire toward the hole in the roof. More family and guests arrive, more than 1,200 from around the world.

The potlatch begins quietly with a subdued greeting in the Kwakwala language, since the crowd is mourning two family members. When women in cloaks and button blankets stand, moving their arms in ritualized movements, they have shaken off the sorrow and are now ready to celebrate. The table and photos are removed and Adam Dick and Daisy Sewid begin the blessing of the floor. Dick moves around the dance area chanting and shaking a white bird wing while Sewid scatters feathers after him. "We believe that spirits still linger," Sewid later explains. "He sings a prayer chant and we use feathers that have been blessed. The feathers represent what we call *nawalakw*, the supernatural spirit. The prayer chants ask the supernatural spirit to come into the Big House."

A drummer moves toward the fire and begins playing. Soon the crowd becomes more animated, as people in the stands start to move in time with the drumming. The mood is more jubilant by the end of the dance when helpers distribute the bags of flour and rice to the assembled guests.

Later, the drumming resumes when elders wearing button blankets and bark head-dresses with ermine trim bring in Harold's oldest daughter dressed in a button blanket, large woven cedar hat and cedar necklace. She is surrounded by a ring of cedar bark. Another elder with blackened face enters and starts to sing. He circles close to the group, and then cuts the bark ring with a knife. After the elders and young woman leave the dance floor, cedar strips are handed out to the crowd to tie around their heads. Sewid explains: "Our people believe that the cedar bark when it is blessed has the *nawalakw* in it and that it brings healing."

Over the two days of the potlatch a memorial pole is dedicated and more than fifty dances are performed. On the second day the dancing is started in the Big House by a young girl in a button blanket. One by one, little dancers in bumblebee masks come out until there are twenty-three, even one in a wheelchair.

Harold Sewid explains to the guests that bumblebees protected his ancestors during the Great Flood. In those days there were huge trees and his ancestors were told to go inside one of them and fix it so that they could survive. When the waters came, the bumblebees flew around the tree and protected them.

Mining

Moving north along the Campbell River waterfront, a deep-sea freighter is loading ore concentrate at the Argonaut Wharf at the base of the spit, carrying on a mining tradition that has been a part of city life since the early 1950s. At that time the Argonaut Company operated an iron mine at Upper Quinsam Lake and built the wharf that still carries its name to load ore onto freighters bound for Japan. Another company, Western Mines, started developing a mine on Myra Creek in Strathcona Park in 1964. Claims first registered in 1918 when the Park Act was amended to allow mining in Strathcona Park permitted Western to plan a mine within BC's oldest provincial park. At one time the mine owners contemplated building a townsite for mine workers in the park but that was dropped after stiff local opposition. Western started the Lynx open-pit mine in 1967. Copper, lead, zinc, gold and silver ore was trucked 90 kilometres (54 miles) away and loaded onto deepwater ships at the Argonaut Wharf. In 1969 Western's Myra underground mine started production and ten years later the HW deposit was discovered nearby, prompting the installation of new infrastructure and an expansion of the milling facilities. Today Breakwater Resources owns the Myra Falls operation, which employs approximately 375 people, two-thirds of them working underground as miners, mechanics, equipment operators, electricians and millwrights. Another company, Cream Silver Mines, tried to open a mine in the park in the '80s but a two-month blockade by the Friends of Strathcona Park and a government

decision to allow no more mines within the park ended the company's plan.

Coal was first discovered in the Campbell River area in 1920, yet mining did not begin until 1987. Originally, the coal was mined by open pit, but in 1994 Quinsam Coal moved its operations underground. Today the low-ash, low-sulphur bituminous thermal coal is trucked to the Middle Point barge facility and then loaded by underground conveyors onto 5,000- to 10,000-tonne barges. The coal from the Quinsam mine is used by power plants in Tacoma, and at cement plants in Richmond and Seattle, where it is burned to heat the kilns. There are plans for mine expansion but elevated sulphate and arsenic levels in Long Lake need to be addressed.

Rowboats in the Tyee Pool just north of the Argonaut Wharf.

The River

It is possible to spend a week in Campbell River today and never see the actual river, but the longer you stay the more you become aware that the river is where the city's soul resides. The Campbell is one of Vancouver Island's largest rivers, arising as it does among the Island's highest mountain range and emptying its largest lake system. In days of yore its bountiful salmon runs attracted a yearly migration of First Nations from the surrounding territory who camped on its broad spit. Early settlers farmed its rich flood plain and the first logging companies found a choice booming ground in its protected estuary. Early too, well-heeled sport fishermen discovered the schools of massive spring salmon that gathered in the shoal off its mouth, the "Tyee Pool" that became a destination for anglers from around the globe by the 1890s and gave the city its claim to being "Salmon Capital of the World."

Preceding pages:
Two fishermen try their luck in
the Campbell River.

The epic beauty of the Campbell watershed caused it to be singled out in 1911 as the location of sprawling 250,000-hectare (625,000-acre) Strathcona Park, British Columbia's first provincial park, but its mineral and hydroelectric wealth made it one of the province's first land-use battlegrounds between industry and conservationists. These conflicts, articulated by the city's great naturalist and author Roderick Haig-Brown, gave Campbell River a place in history as the cradle of the west coast environmental movement, which in time spread around the world under the banner of Greenpeace.

Mike King, one of the pioneer loggers in the area, realized the hydro potential of Elk Falls on the Campbell River back in the 1890s, and formed the Campbell River Power Company with the idea of providing power to a townsite he staked out at Duncan Bay, 4 kilometres (2.5 miles) north of the river mouth. King staked the townsite on the strength of a proposed trans-continental rail line. The rail line was to reach the mainland coast at Bute Inlet, cross Quadra Island to Vancouver Island just north of Duncan Bay and then continue down to Victoria. The railway proposal failed when surveyors found that additional islands, namely, Sonora and Maurelle, would have to be crossed rather than just Quadra.

However, Mike King's dream of harnessing Elk Falls finally became a reality when Premier John Hart switched on the generators at the John Hart Dam in 1947. In 1951 the BC Power Commission began work on the second dam, Ladore, located farther up the river system on Lower Campbell Lake. When it was announced there was to be a third dam in Strathcona Park, Roderick Haig-Brown and others voiced concern over how the wilderness values of the park would be affected, especially trout spawning areas in Buttle Lake. Labelled the Battle of the Buttle, this was one of the first major conservation confrontations in BC. Four years of protest from Haig-Brown and fish and game associations succeeded in having the third dam located on Upper Campbell Lake rather than Buttle Lake. This raised the water level on Buttle Lake 6 metres (20 feet) and flooded the shoreline, but Haig-Brown felt that the damage would have been worse without public action.

Opposite: Elk Falls, where the
Campbell River drops 25 metres
into a rock-walled canyon, has
been featured in several movies.

The John Hart Dam had unexpected consequences for the health of the salmon spawning in the Campbell River. Dave Ewart, manager of the Quinsam Hatchery, said that one of the biggest challenges to Campbell River salmon is the shortage of gravel for spawning. "For seventy years they used to dredge the river mouth to facilitate log booming and the dam prevents the downstream migration of gravel." A special gravel committee was instrumental in having spawning gravel placed in the river and spawning channels created alongside the river.

Quinsam Hatchery

The Quinsam River flows into the Campbell River about a kilometre upstream from the highway bridges. Each year, five species of Pacific salmon (chinook, coho, pink, chum and a small number of sockeye) and two species of sea-run trout (steelhead and cutthroat) return to the Quinsam and Campbell rivers to spawn. Generally, the salmon spawn in the fall and the trout in the spring. The preferred time to observe salmon is when they are spawning in large numbers and easily seen from shore from September to November. Adult salmon are found throughout the river, but the largest concentration is usually just below the hatchery that was built in 1974 on the Quinsam.

1

Top: A friendly guide prepares to take snorkellers upstream for their first swim with the salmon.

Right: A snorkeller drifts down the Campbell River through schools of pink and coho salmon heading upstream.

Bottom: Excited snorkellers try to describe the size of the chinook they've seen on their float down the Campbell River.

At the hatchery eggs are taken from ripe females and fertilized with the milt from the males. The eggs are kept in trays with a constant source of water until they hatch and start to feed. The hatchery is varying release times into the ocean to see if it has an effect on the number of returning salmon.

Counting Salmon

On a beautiful fall afternoon the hatchery enumeration crew, a team of divers trained to swim the river and estimate numbers of spawning salmon, gears up. Water levels in the river are determined by the John Hart Dam and today the crew are checking to see if they are adequate for chinook spawning. The previous week, when the crew had swum the river, the water levels were so shallow they had to crawl on hands and knees down a spawning channel. If levels are too low for spawning salmon, BC Hydro will release more water.

After donning dry-suits, the crew drive up to the generating station just below the canyon leading from Elk Falls. Pulling on hoods, gloves and fins they slide into the river and swim upstream into the shadowy waters of the canyon. Schools of salmon dart about in the depths of the canyon pool.

Once the crew start swimming downstream the adrenaline kicks in. It takes training to recognize different fish species, concentrate on counting and still be ready for constantly changing river conditions. Some of the salmon have obviously been caught by fishers and escaped as they have lures hanging from their mouths. A fisherman yells at one of the divers for coming too close to his line. Later, during a debriefing session at the hatchery, the divers estimate they saw 2,300 chinook in the river. Dave Ewart explains that some of the fish counted by the crew were on their way to spawn in the Quinsam River. Before the dam was built an estimated 4,000 chinook spawned in the Campbell River, and in the last twenty years with reduced habitat the number has averaged around 700. Several companies provide guided snorkel trips down shorter sections of the river so visitors can experience the wonder of swimming with the salmon for themselves.

A Quinsam Hatchery worker removes eggs from a returning salmon. Ian Douglas photo

Hudson Farm

Rivermouth Farm is home to the Hudsons, a third-generation Campbell River family. Tom Hudson left England after agricultural college and came to the coast in the 1920s looking for farmland. When he got to Campbell River he found lodging at the Painter family fishing camp on Tyee Spit. They told him about a parcel of land across the Campbell River estuary that was the site of an old logging camp. Hudson bought the land and started to split cedar rails for fences and move rocks with his horse and sled. In 1935 he married Mavis Hyde and they had two children.

Diana Kretz, Tom Hudson's daughter, remembers going across Discovery Passage to the cannery store at Quathiaski Cove on Quadra Island to buy ice cream in a boat her father built. "Campbell River in the '40s was a time of barter, trading eggs for groceries. Once the pulp mill came, after the dam was built in the '50s, this whole thing became a boom town. People had money; there were big bunkhouses for the construction crews."

The Hudson farm has been growing pumpkins for Halloween for years and Diana's daughter Connie has continued the family farming tradition by starting a vegetable business.

Painter's Lodge

The original Painter's Lodge began as a series of tents on the Tyee Spit in 1922. Ned Painter built rental rowboats that were hired out with a tyee guide, and his wife June provided accommodation and meals. The Painters bought land on the north side of the river from Tom Hudson and built a Tudor-style lodge in 1929 that was popular with the rich and famous who came to row for salmon. Ned and June Painter sold the lodge in 1948 and it burnt down in 1985 under suspicious circumstances. A disgruntled employee might have had something to do with the fire but charges were never laid. The Oak Bay Marine Group, a company that owns marinas and sportfishing lodges throughout BC, built the new Painter's Lodge on the property. Today the resort has 94 rooms in six wings and the main lodge features a dining room, pub, lounge and gift shop. The major draw is the guided sport fishing but there is a pool, hot tubs, tennis courts, fitness centre, whale watching and other activities such as the "Painters at Painter's" weekend. Every May an invited group of painters share their talents and give lectures to a sell-out crowd of art lovers.

The Tyee Club

First Nations harvested the run of large fish that returned to the Campbell River for thousands of years. The first account of angling for tyee—chinook salmon weighing more than 14 kilograms or 30 pounds—appeared in *The Field*, in London, in October 1896. Sir Richard Musgrave, a British naval officer who married into Vancouver Island's wealthy Dunsmuir family, wrote about fishing the mouth of Campbell River from a dugout canoe paddled by a Native guide. His largest fish weighed 32 kilograms (70 pounds). Five years later one angler described his nineteen days of fishing in Campbell River under the title "Two Tons of Salmon with the Rod." His lightest salmon weighed in at 22.5 pounds and the heaviest at 58 pounds. These stories started a gold

Top: The world-famous Painter's Fishing Lodge began as tents on the Tyee Spit in the 1920s and later moved into buildings across the river. When it burned down in 1985, the Oak Bay Marine Group built a new Painter's Lodge.

Above: A young employee at Painter's Lodge displays a chinook salmon caught in the waters around Quadra Island.

Above: The famous Tyee Club sign with its signature bell that signals when a tyee has been officially weighed.

Left: Fishers from abroad hired the expert services of First Nations fishermen.
Carl Thulin Collection, Museum of Campbell River
10215

rush among world-travelling sport fishermen who were drawn to the area with the hopes of fighting and landing one of these giants. After World War I there was such a sharp increase in the number of tyee fishermen that local anglers became concerned about the sustainability of the resource.

The Tyee Club of British Columbia was formed in Campbell River in the summer of 1924 by Dr. J.A. Wiborn of California; Melville Haigh, manager of the Willows Hotel; and A.N. Wolverton of Vancouver. It was modelled after the famous Catalina Island Tuna Club, which has as its motto "fair play for game fishes." Fish were only to be caught from a rowboat in the waters of Discovery Passage, on a line with a breaking strength of 20 pounds or less, on a rod between six and nine feet long, with a hand-operated single-action reel and either a spoon or a plug.

An annual Championship Button and title of "Tyee Man" is awarded to the fisherman who lands the largest salmon. A bronze button is awarded for a 30- to 40-pound fish, a silver button for a 40- to 50-pound fish, a gold button for a 50- to 60-pound fish, and a diamond button for a fish over 60 pounds. A booklet recording the results of the year's fishing is published annually, and daily updates are available on the Tyee Club website.

The Pulp Mill

Continuing up the highway through industrial North Campbell River past Painter's Lodge, a side road leads to Duncan Bay, site of the sprawling Elk Falls pulp mill. In 1947 Crown Zellerbach Canada Ltd., a major world supplier of paper that had a pulp mill operating in Ocean Falls on the mid-coast, announced a partnership with Comox Logging and Railway Company and the Canadian Western Lumber Company to build a pulp mill in Duncan Bay.

The partnership acquired a long-term licence to harvest pulp wood—logs that are

Rowing for Tyee

To fully understand the mystique of the Tyee Club I make arrangements to go rowing early one morning with my cousin John, who spent his teenage years guiding for salmon in the area. In the pre-dawn darkness he picks me up in his dinghy. The first tyee rowboats, long with graceful lines, were built by Ned Painter when the family ran a fishing camp on Tyee Spit. We motor down to just off the end of the spit. Once there, as regulated, John shuts off the outboard. As he rows toward the clubhouse we are in the Tyee Pool, an area where the large chinook gather before ascending the river. He tells me to let out 12 pulls of line (about 24 feet/7 metres). After attaching a lead weight he instructs me to let out double the original amount of line. We are using an 8-foot 10-inch (2.7-metre) rod and a reel filled with 18-pound test line. His son had given him a pink plug that has already caught several tyee.

John tells me to flip the rod over so the reel is on the top and then place my thumb on the reel so I can deliver a solid strike. "When the fish hits I want you to strike it and get your hand out of the way and let the fish run. Don't hesitate on the strike. They hit the plugs hard."

Early morning light silhouettes tyee fishermen out in their rowboats in Discovery Passage.

There are about thirty boats out rowing this morning, many with their running lights still glowing. Amid the cry of gulls, and the squeak of oarlocks, there is an occasional greeting. We notice the odd boat head out into Discovery Passage. Once a fish is on, John will row us out of the pool, away from the other anglers.

Forty years ago rowing for salmon was quite formal. "People only spoke in whispers," John informs me. "Now things are more casual, and there are a lot more boats on the water. When we started there were only guides and guests from the nearby fishing resort of Painter's Lodge and maybe three or four locals."

He says for a time rowing fell out of fashion but, after local physician Doc Murphy took a mould off a wooden rowboat and fibreglass rowboats became available, the sport found new life. "Certainly at nighttime there can be sixty or seventy rowboats out here. Bit of a gong show."

John starts rowing faster; we are on at the end of the pool and have to turn around to stay in the area where the fish are waiting to go up the river. Suddenly three boats have fish on around us.

"Whoa!" The reel screams as a big fish takes my plug. I haul back on the rod to set the hook. The screech of the reel means we have a solid fish on. John tells me to flip the rod over now the hook is set. As he rows us away from the rest of the fleet I ask nervously for tips on how best to play the fish.

After six minutes of strong runs alternating with frantic reeling, John says, "I can see the pink plug." With the fish near the surface, he readies the net, but the fish has other ideas and rockets off on one last run.

A few minutes later a 20-pound (9-kilogram) chinook has been netted and lies in the bottom of the boat. If the fish had been larger, close to tyee size, we would have taken it to the clubhouse to be weighed. We hear a commotion and look ashore to see people dancing as their fish is being weighed, followed by three strokes of the bell, confirmation that a tyee has been landed. We hear someone shout "Thirty-two and a half… I've got blood in the boat."

The sun is up, and as we pack up the gear John greets fellow anglers. "Top of the morning, Mr. and Mrs. Berger. We got an undersize, no joy on the bell."

Freighters from around the world tie up for their loads of paper products from the Elk Falls mill.

too small or of too low quality to be sawn up for lumber—for the mill. The mill opened in 1952 and was the major employer in Campbell River for over half a century. To feed the massive mill there was a constant stream of barges and a sawmill operated nearby; the tall stacks belched acrid fumes that some call the "smell of money." Young men graduating from high school could always get a job there. The mill expanded and changed owners several times. In February 2009, during a global economic downturn and depressed market for newsprint, the mill was idled by its current owners, Catalyst Paper Corporation. All indications are the shutdown is permanent.

Campbell River People

Fred Nunns

One of the first Europeans to settle in the Campbell River area was Fred Nunns, an Irish bachelor with an unruly handlebar moustache and a good diary habit. Nunns cleared land and built a log cabin about a mile up the Campbell River in 1888 with the idea of selling vegetables and animals to local logging camps. His diary describes a typical day in the coastal homesteader's life. He loaded his canoe with pumpkins to sell at a camp on the top end of Quadra Island, stopping partway to camp overnight. He misjudged the rising tide and when he awoke his canoe was overturned, the bay bobbing with pumpkins. He salvaged what he could and continued to the camp, only to find the loggers preoccupied with a drunken party that kept him awake all night. The next morning he was able to sell his pumpkins for 37 cents each, which he promptly spent on five bags of crushed barley for his hogs, one dozen bullets and three bottles of meat sauce. To his great delight, he also succeeded in borrowing twenty books, his only source of entertainment. When Fred's sister and three brothers arrived from the homeland they took out more land and built the two-storey, seven-room Padeswood,

One of Campbell River's first non-Native settlers, Fred Nunns (left) receives a visitor, thought to be surveyor Drabble of Courtenay. Ruth (Pidcock) Barnett Collection, Museum of Campbell River 6910

complete with a piano transported from Comox precariously balanced between two canoes. The siblings lasted only two years before moving on, leaving Fred to lament to his diary, "So I will be here alone." He endured another thirty years, selling land to the growing town and cultivating his eccentricities. A boarder reported, "He got up in the morning, lit the kitchen stove and put on a pot of porridge. Then, still in his pyjamas and slippers, he placed a straw hat on his head, walked down to the river, waded into a deep pool up to his neck, took off his hat and ducked his head under the water." This was his daily ritual. After all those years of dodging bears on lonely trails and defying death in tidal rapids, he died in 1920 during a visit to the dentist.

Lord Hughie Horatio Nelson Baron Bacon

Hugh H.N.B. Bacon, "Lord B" for short, was a trapper and prospector with a cabin on Buttle Lake with this sign in front:

Hugh H.N.B. Bacon, shown here at Gowlland Harbour, 1917. Mary (Hall) Ritter Collection, Museum of Campbell River 16721

> BEWARE
> Tread these forest Isles
> Softly
> Do not disturb the great
> Forest and storm God
> Lord Bacon, The only Lord in America

Bacon would appear in his tattered rags at the Willows Hotel and go on three-day benders during which he would entertain bemused locals by declaiming passages from the classics in plummy British accents that bespoke an expensive upper-class education gone for naught. But the Lord had his serious side. "He would suddenly sober down," wrote visiting angler Sir John Rogers, "and though wizened in appearance, he would put a pack on his back only a few men could carry and disappear into the woods to his lonely cabin, only to reappear in a few days ready for a fresh spree." Bacon put his grimy thumbprint on history when he served as guide for the Price Ellison expedition tasked with appraising the Strathcona Park proposal in 1910, expertly leading a hapless crew of lawyers, politicians, social butterflies and overweight servants on a gruelling survey of the region's top attractions. He should perhaps be considered the area's original environmentalist.

The Thulin Brothers

The Campbell River operation began as a joint venture by both Thulins, Charles and his younger brother Fred, and at first they commuted across the strait from Lund, leaving a manager in charge. As Campbell River grew, they agreed on a division of labour, with Charlie moving his family to the Island while Fred held the fort on the mainland

Above: Fred Thulin's portrait, ca. 1920s, hung in the Lund Hotel. Powell River Historical Museum & Archives ND010436

Left: Charles and Mary Thulin with children, Anna, Elin, Carl and baby Lillie, ca. 1900. Florence Thulin Collection, Museum of Campbell River 15432

side, both becoming revered as "Poppa Thulin" in their respective communities. They were ideal founders—imaginative, bold and industrious but also very public-spirited. At Christmas Charlie and Mary would invite everyone to the hotel for dinner, and seldom missed a chance to host a community gathering, particularly on July 1. Charlie was a stocky, good-natured man with a bit of a stammer and a favourite target for pranks. One particular layabout named George Verdier became so expert at imitating Poppa's Swedish drawl he could fool anyone, even Mrs. Thulin. Once he pretended to be Charlie in the act of loudly seducing a lady guest in one of the hotel rooms as Mary was passing by. A short time later Charlie stomped into the bar, and coming as close as he could to violence, seized Verdier by the shoulder and lectured him, "Now... now... now... now Yorge, that was no yoke, you know, the Old Woman, she's madder than hell!" Charlie's fatal flaw was an excess of generosity. When it came to granting credit he just couldn't say no, and by 1923 the Thulins were owed thousands of dollars they couldn't collect. Even the hospital owed them three thousand dollars it couldn't pay. Finally their own creditors called their debts and in 1923 the Thulins were out of business, both in Campbell River and Lund. In the end the assets were sold for enough to cover the debts and leave the family with some property, which served to launch a second generation of Thulins in business. Charlie and Mary's daughter Lillie became one of the town's early real estate developers; her brother Carl and his wife Margaret started the Bee Hive Café, a Campbell River landmark to this day, and Pioneer Hardware, which is still in the family.

Cecil Smith (left), cougar bounty hunter and guide, honed his skills while growing up in Black Creek in the 1890s. Margaret (Pidcock) Dunn Collection, Museum of Campbell River 11538

Cecil "Cougar" Smith

It took long days to clear land and during the night cougars occasionally took a liking to a pig or raided the chicken coop. Cecil "Cougar" Smith grew up in Black Creek where he learned to track animals searching for lost cattle. He shot his first cougar at 14 and became famous as a bounty hunter and hunting guide. By 1920 he reckoned he had dispatched more than a thousand cougars, 150 just from the area around the Big Rock. He served as a predator control officer for the Province from 1919 to 1939 and later earned a reputation as a tyee guide.

David Vanstone

David Vanstone was the opposite of the eccentric, overbred kind of English immigrant typified by "Lord" Hughie Bacon. His first job in BC was as driver of a honey wagon emptying outhouses in Victoria before he became a boss logger on Quadra Island with a formidable reputation as a brawler. It is said he lost only one fight—to the legendary Skookum Tom Leask, reputedly the strongest man on the coast. He was also known as an elegant ballroom dancer. He was still a vigorous fifty when he retired from logging to become a farmer in North Campbell River and it wasn't long before he was up to his neck in business. He began by buying the Thulins' big general store when the creditors sold it off in the early 1920s, developed property north of the river and in the 1930s built several business blocks that still stand in downtown Campbell River. Remembered for his strong community spirit and charitable habits, he was officially anointed as Charlie Thulin's successor as community leader in 1935.

David Vanstone (right) and his wife, Eliza (centre), with her cousin Mary Watson, at their home on the beach at the end of Vanstone Road, ca. 1936. Ramona Vanstone Collection, Museum of Campbell River 18432

Roderick Haig-Brown

Roderick Haig-Brown (February 21, 1908 – October 9, 1976) was one of Canada's

most widely read essayists and nature writers. A more recent local writer observed that since both Campbell River newspapers regularly run pieces by Haig-Brown you might be excused for thinking he was still alive and scribbling. The remarkable thing is that opinion pieces Haig-Brown wrote half a century ago about the conservation ethic and the importance of intact ecosystems seem to make more sense with each passing year.

Haig-Brown grew up at his grandfather's estate in Dorset where he acquired a life-long passion for the outdoors. He decided to travel until he was old enough to join the Foreign Service and in 1926 made his way across the States to the US Pacific Northwest. When his US visa ran out he came to Canada and went up to the Nimpkish Valley on the north end of Vancouver Island where he worked as a logger, commercial fisherman and fish guide. When he returned to England it seemed tame after the wilds of BC so in 1931 Haig-Brown came back to Campbell River, married Ann Elmore of Seattle, bought "Above Tide," a homestead on the banks of the Campbell River, raised three daughters and one son and wrote 23 books. His life in Campbell River is chronicled in the elegant memoir, *Measure of the Year*.

Some people around Campbell River remember Haig-Brown best as a magistrate. He had no legal training but in those days the government would appoint anybody with reasonable reading skills and a clean record to hear cases in police court. Haig-Brown made a career of it, forging a reputation as a fair and considerate judge—but not someone you wanted to appear before on anything to do with the environment. His dedication to the environment led him into political activism at times, notably in opposing the plan to put a hydroelectric dam on Buttle Lake in the early 1950s, a campaign that marked the birth of the BC environmental movement.

John Grant, a Quadra lawyer, worked with Haig-Brown and admired his writing.

"I had read *Saltwater Summer, Silver, Panther, Starbuck Valley Winter*," said Grant. "I found the lifestyle that he described—commercial fishing in the summer, hunting deer in the winter, sport fishing—very appealing to a city kid like me. He described a coast way of life I had never seen."

Haig-Brown was among the first to start snorkelling the river to observe the behaviour of the salmon in their own element. Grant went around to his house one day to find Haig-Brown in a wetsuit. "You wouldn't believe it," said Haig-Brown, "you get in the river and the fish just treat you like one of their own. It's magic, you don't see how the fish operate when you are above the water, and your vision is refracted."

The Haig-Browns sold their property to the Province of BC in 1975 and it was dedicated as a historic site in 1990. In the fall a Roderick Haig-Brown Festival is held on the grounds with fly-tying and fly-fishing demonstrations, river rafting, nature walks, awards for local conservation work and readings from Haig-Brown's many books. In the winter there is a writer-in-residence program that brings in writers from across the country. In summer you can stay at Above Tide, which is run as a B&B, and wander through the library where Haig-Brown wrote so eloquently about fly fishing and the rhythms of the changing seasons.

Local Hero Rod Brind'Amour

Rod Brind'Amour (b. 1970) was an outstanding National Hockey League player who was raised in Campbell River and played his early hockey in local rinks. He played college hockey at Michigan State before St. Louis took him ninth overall in the 1988 NHL entry draft. He was traded to the Philadelphia Flyers in 1991 and then to the Carolina Hurricanes in 2000. He played in the 1992 NHL All-Star Game, won the Frank J. Selke Award for best defensive forward twice and played for Canada in the 1998 Olympics. His best year was 1992–93 when he scored 97 points; he scored 70 points or more eight times—not bad for a defensive specialist. He became captain of the Hurricanes and won the Stanley Cup with them in 2006. That summer there was a parade through downtown Campbell River as he brought the cup home and the town named Brind'Amour Road in his honour. When he retired in 2010 after playing an impressive 1,484 games and scoring 1,184 points over 21 seasons, the Hurricanes announced they would retire his number 17 jersey. He is considered a shoo-in for the Hockey Hall of Fame. During his playing days Brind'Amour was nicknamed "Rod the Bod" in recognition of his penchant for intensive physical conditioning, a factor in allowing him to play at such a high level for so many years.

The Rod Brind'Amour Charity Golf Tournament started in 1995 when Kim Black, a 14-year-old cystic fibrosis patient, asked Brind'Amour to come home for a fundraiser. He agreed on two conditions: first, all the money raised had to go to CF research; and second, the event had to be organized in such a way that he would be proud to be its patron. The annual event has been a major success on both counts.

Campbell River's famous son, Rod Brind'Amour. Gregg Forwerck, Carolina Hurricanes photo

The Arts

The Henderson Family

On the shore beside the Argonaut Wharf a family of woodcarvers and printmakers create works of art in the Henderson family carving shed. Many of the totem poles in Campbell River were carved by Bill Henderson, his late father Sam or Bill's deceased brother Ernie. Mark, another brother, has specialized in prints that are sold around the world. He also painted the Campbell River Band Big House exterior along with nephews Greg and Junior, and the interior wall in Tsa-Kwa-Luten Lodge on nearby Quadra Island.

The family patriarch, Sam Henderson, was born in Seymour Inlet in 1905. His father was a Scots steam engineer on the *Grappler*, a coastal steamer that caught fire and sank in Seymour Narrows in 1883. Taken in by local First Nations, Sam's father married Lucy Johnson. Sam moved to Campbell River in 1929 and five years later married May Quocksister, the eldest daughter of Chief John Quocksister. Sam and May had sixteen children and in the cedar-scented carving shed Bill and Mark carry on their father's creative legacy.

Above: Master carver Bill Henderson takes a break in his carving shed by the cruise ship terminal. Bill has sold his work to collectors around the world.

Left: A sun mask carved by Bill Henderson hangs in the Campbell River Museum. It opens and closes, revealing a second mask within.

Sybil Andrews

Sybil Andrews was already internationally famous for her linocuts when she immigrated to Canada and settled in Campbell River in 1947. Born in Bury St. Edmunds, England, in 1898, she worked as a welder in an aircraft assembly line during World War I. She took a correspondence art course and had her first exhibition of watercolours and pastels in 1921. Her linocut prints first appeared in the 12th International Print Makers Exhibition in Los Angeles in 1931 and were exhibited around the world. During World War II she met Walter M. Morgan, a co-worker in the British Power Boat shipyard, and they were married in 1943.

After they arrived in Campbell River Sybil taught music and art in her small studio. Walter started a boat-building business and worked at the Elk Falls Mill.

Walter died in 1986 and Sybil four years later. A year before she passed away, Sybil donated 575 works to the Glenbow Museum in Calgary and later bequeathed 960 works that include all of her famous colour linocuts and the original linoleum blocks, paintings in oil and watercolour, drawings, drypoint etchings, sketchbooks and personal papers.

The City of Campbell River purchased Sybil's cottage in 1997. After it was declared a "Legacy Landmark" the Campbell River Community Arts Council moved in. The Council sponsors the very popular Banner Project, which started in 1994. Elementary and high school students as well as artists in the community produce cloth banners that are hung from light standards throughout the city. In the fall the banners are exhibited in the lobby of the Tidemark Theatre and sold by silent auction. The Arts Council hosts a joint member show in the Tidemark Theatre lobby and a student art show and annual photography show in February.

Chainsaw Art—Transformations on the Shore

One of Campbell River's more distinctive cultural events is the Transformations on the Shore Chainsaw Carving Contest. In 1996, well-known First Nation artist Max Chickite used his chainsaw to carve an octopus from an old beach stump and left it for all to admire on the foreshore. Vandals cut off the octopus's head, which was found a few days later on a logging road. Chickite repaired the charred, damaged head and returned it to the octopus's body. The vandalism caused such a furor that a driftwood-carving competition was started. This turned into the Transformations on the Shore Chainsaw Carving Contest, which is held in Frank James Park, close by the Sybil Andrews Cottage. The annual five-day contest attracts up to thirty carvers from around BC and beyond to compete in novice, amateur and professional levels. Savvy spectators avail themselves of the earplugs on offer as there is a cacophony of engine noise while the chainsaws slice away. Some carvers have made the switch to electric saws and woodworking grinders but the majority remain faithful to their STIHLs and Husqvarnas. On the last day of the competition there is a Quick Carve competition where the artists have an hour to carve a masterpiece to be auctioned off.

Danny Richey, Transformations winning carver entry 2007.

Campbell River Art Gallery

Doris Ritchie and fellow Arts Council members opened the Campbell River Art Gallery in 1994 in the Centenary Building downtown. Twenty unique exhibitions a year are chosen by a panel and there is one non-juried members show that attracts entries

Bongo Love working on his entry in the Transformations on the Shore woodcarving contest.

Above: Local author Jeanette Taylor is the executive director of the Campbell River Art Gallery.

Left: Friendly faces at the visitor information office in the Campbell River Art Gallery greet visitors and offer helpful suggestions for an exciting experience in the area.

from sixty to eighty local artists. There is an art rental program as well as a teaching studio where courses are held throughout the year.

Performing Arts

An integral part of the downtown core is the handsomely restored Tidemark Theatre. The original Van Isle Movie Theatre opened in 1947 and the art deco structure was feeling its age when the building was purchased by the City in 1985. A group of volunteers fundraised to convert the theatre into a performing arts centre over the next two years. Work included removing several rows of seating to build a proper stage and rebuilding the projectionist booth into a control room. A non-profit society runs the theatre for the City of Campbell River.

Around Town

Strathcona Park

Strathcona Provincial Park, designated in 1911, is the oldest provincial park in British Columbia. A rugged mountain wilderness comprising more than 250,000 hectares (615,000 acres), it covers the centre of the island 48 kilometres (30 miles) southwest of Campbell River. Della Falls, the highest waterfall in Canada with an overall drop of 440 metres (1,450 feet) in three cascades, is located in the southern section of the park. Strathcona was originally surveyed with the idea of developing a Banff-style park with large hotels. It was established after a 23-member expedition led by Price Ellison, then Minister of Lands in the BC government under Premier Richard McBride, left Campbell River on July 7, 1910, and proceeded up the Campbell Lakes chain, climbing Crown Mountain northwest of Buttle Lake. A road from Campbell River was built partway into the park but the hotel project was abandoned when World War I started. Over the years visitor facilities have been developed in the Paradise Meadow/Forbidden Plateau area for skiing and hiking, and Strathcona Park Lodge on Upper Campbell Lake offers kayaking and climbing. Jim and Myrna Boulding opened the original Strathcona Park Lodge in 1959 while

A school group from Strathcona Park Lodge learns to climb at the Crest Creek training area.

they were both still teachers at Carihi Secondary School. Their dream was to develop an outdoor education centre and over the years thousands of students have learned outdoor skills at this facility on the shores of Upper Campbell Lake. Jim passed away in 1986, and Myrna continues to operate the lodge with her oldest son, Jamie.

Preceding pages: Climbers enjoy the view from the top of Elkhorn Mountain in Strathcona Park, the second highest peak on Vancouver Island.

Ripple Rock (the other Big Rock)

Ripple Rock took more than a hundred lives before the killer rock was blown up in the world's largest non-nuclear blast in 1958. Ripple Rock lurked only 3 metres (9 feet) below the surface of Seymour Narrows, a passage only 1 kilometre (half a mile) wide between Vancouver Island and Quadra, 14 kilometres (9 miles) north of Campbell River. At peak tides the water rushes through the Narrows at 15 knots (17 mph), creating large whirlpools that have capsized loaded fishboats. The USS *Saranac* was the first recorded shipwreck in 1875. The side-wheel steamer attempted a passage at low tide against the advice of the pilot. "We struck a sunken rock with tremendous force that threw almost everyone standing from his feet to one side," wrote survivor J.A. Kelley, "and it seemed for some moments that she would turn over entirely." The forward deck was bent upward like a sheet of paper, and although everyone made it into boats and onto the Quadra shore, they had to wait a week for rescue.

More than one hundred vessels were wrecked or damaged on Ripple Rock before an attempt

Workers tunnelled under the twin peaks of Ripple Rock and set explosives to blast off the top of the marine hazard in Seymour Narrows on April 5, 1958. R.E. Olsen photo, Vancouver *Province* Collection, Museum of Campbell River 12150

was made to get rid of it during World War II. On the first attempt in 1943 a 46-metre (150-foot) drilling barge was anchored over the reef with 3.8-centimetre (1.5-inch) steel cables. It took 24 hours for the first cable to snap and they continued to break until engineers fastened the barge to Vancouver Island with overhead cables. The attempt was abandoned after a summer and in 1945 another drilling barge was positioned over Ripple Rock with overhead cables. Once again the current proved too strong, and a crew boat capsized, drowning nine workers. Finally the government got serious and hatched a plan to dig a tunnel out from shore and attack the infamous hazard from below. A causeway was built from Quadra to Maude Island, the point of land nearest Ripple Rock, a vertical shaft was sunk 174 metres (570 feet) then a horizontal one was drifted 762 metres (2,500 feet) across the narrows and up into Ripple Rock. Sixty miners based in a camp on Quadra worked round-the-clock shifts for two years to complete the tunnelling. The charge chambers were packed with 1,237 tonnes (1,375 tons) of Nitramex 2H explosive and on April 5, 1958, the RCMP blocked roads in a 5-kilometre (3-mile) radius of the blast site as film crews and special guests including 89-year-old logging pioneer R.D. Merrill hunkered down in an observation bunker on Maude Island. At 9:31.02 a.m. 330,000 tonnes (370,000 tons) of rock erupted into the sky, removing the hazard once and for all. Fretful talk of mega-quakes being triggered and tsunamis flooding homes, which had some Campbell River residents poised in idling cars, proved groundless as no effects worse than a faint tremor reached town. This was one of the first live television broadcasts in Canada and for thousands marked their first experience of TV. The photo of the blast plume at full height went iconic, becoming one of the most recognized and frequently reproduced images in Canadian history.

Today hikers can look down on the site where the rock still lurks a harmless 15 metres (50 feet) below the surface by taking the 4-kilometre (2.5-mile) Ripple Rock Trail from the marked trailhead 15.5 kilometres (9.5 miles) north of town to the Seymour Narrows lookout, which offers views across to Quadra and Maude islands.

Brown's Bay

Located 19 kilometres (12 miles) north of Campbell River, Brown's Bay Marina is a popular fishing harbour. The land was logged just after World War I when small mines were still being worked in the area. Marion and Milt Adams bought the land and started a family fishing resort, then sold to Alec Baikie who developed an RV park with a clubhouse on the shoreline behind the marina. Today, a popular chum salmon fishing derby in the fall draws over five hundred entrants and has contributed more than $24,000 to the Greenways Land Trust, a Campbell River organization that coordinates stream stewardship projects and maintains the trails in the Beaver Lodge Lands.

Brown's Bay Packing Company, located beside the marina, started processing farmed salmon in 1989. The company chose the site because it is easily accessed by boats delivering salmon from the farms. With an initial staff of 25 and a modestly sized facility, Brown's Bay Packing originally hoped to process 2.5 million pounds of farmed fresh salmon for markets in the US and Canada. Today they have 45 full-time people and process in excess of 32 million pounds of product a year.

Sayward–Kelsey Bay

Located on Johnstone Strait, 74 kilometres (46 miles) north of Campbell River, the small village of Sayward (population 341) is one of the oldest in the region. Elder Ruby Wilson remembers that it was once the site of a major K'omoks village. "My grandmother often told me the story of a young woman, a prophetess who lived long ago at the Salmon River village of H'kusam. She said that there were going to be strange people coming around… in huge canoes, not like ours, and that one day there would be nobody left at the village. A lot of the people didn't believe that because Salmon River was one of the biggest villages on the coast at that time; the biggest and the strongest."

The Salmon River runs through the town of Sayward and empties into the ocean at Kelsey Bay.

A young man takes a music break while attending an outdoor course at Strathcona Park Lodge.

The Cable Cook House and Café, a landmark restaurant in Sayward built out of old logging cable, is known for its large, home-cooked meals.

One of the first non-Native settlements at Kelsey Bay was the Sacht family farm of the 1890s at Sayward.
Royal BC Museum, BC Archives D-02365

After being devastated both by their Laichwiltach neighbours and European diseases, villagers made the prophecy come true by abandoning the site in 1917. This was well after one of the first non-Native settlers, Otto Sacht, took out his pre-emption in the 1890s, cleared a small farm and in 1904 opened a trading post, two years before the Thulins set up in Campbell River. Like most of coastal settlements that began in a dream of farming, Sayward found its true vocation in the forest industry, becoming home to some early railway operations eventually taken over by MacMillan Bloedel, which established log sorts and booming grounds at Kelsey Bay and Eve River. The Village of Sayward was established as a company townsite to house MacMillan Bloedel's employees and was incorporated in 1968. Weyerhaeuser's purchase of MacMillan Bloedel in 1999 resulted in the closure of both the Eve River and Kelsey Bay log sorts.

Kelsey Bay harbour is the only small craft harbour located between Campbell River and Port McNeill on Johnstone Strait. It served as the southern terminus for the BC Ferries Inside Passage route until 1978, when Highway 19 was extended north to Port Hardy, and remains a convenient stopping point for sport fishing and eco-tourism. It offers a loading ramp, derrick, breakwater, and marine gas. Fresh seafood is often available from one or more boats tied up at the wharf.

One of the popular stops for motorists visiting Sayward is a unique building known as the Cable Cook House, home of the Cable Café. Built by Glen Duncan, a pioneer logger, the walls are entirely covered with 2,500 metres (8,200 feet) of wire rope welded to the iron frame of the structure. The weight of these walls is an impressive 23 tonnes (26 tons).

Fishermen experience the thrill of a double header, with two fish on at one time.

2

Quadra Island

For many years Quadra was known as Valdes Island, which also applied to Maurelle and Sonora. It was not until 1903 that Quadra was renamed in memory of a different Spanish explorer, Juan Francisco de la Bodega y Quadra, whose name had originally been attached to Vancouver Island.

Growing up on Quadra gave Al Luoma, now the Granite Bay Park attendant, a unique outlook on life.

Twenty-one kilometres (13 miles) long and 9.6 kilometres (6 miles) wide, Quadra Island packs a lot of magic into a small space. The north section of the island is rocky and forested with provincial parks full of lakes best explored by canoe, tiny coves perfect for a kayak and secluded anchorages suitable for larger yachts. In contrast, the southern section of the island where most of the 3,500 inhabitants have settled is more level. Settlement is concentrated in three areas, the Cape Mudge village on the very south end and the two business centres on the island, Quathiaski Cove and Heriot Bay, which provide all the amenities one would expect in a rural community.

Back in the late 1800s the government promoted Quadra and neighbouring Cortes, Read, Sonora and Maurelle islands as agricultural paradises. Many homesteaders, however, found the soils and climate were more suited to growing trees than cash crops. The government pre-emption plan allowed settlers to buy 64 hectares (160 acres) for one dollar an acre as long as they made improvements such as clearing the land, fencing fields and building a home. In 1885 Charles Dallas became the first non-Native settler, establishing a ranch close to the present Heriot Bay Inn. After the coastal steamers started making weekly stops in 1892, four distinct communities developed: Quathiaski Cove, Heriot Bay on the east side of the island, Bold Point just north of Heriot Bay and Granite Bay on the northwest corner of the island. By 1910 both Heriot

A winding driveway embodies the rural aspect of life on Quadra Island.

Bay and Quathiaski Cove had more than a hundred inhabitants. Heriot Bay had a hotel, store and a sawmill. A cannery started in 1904 in Quathiaski Cove where there was a store, sawmill, post office, county courthouse and jail. Campbell River's few settlers would row across to Quathiaski Cove for mail and supplies. The fledgling village of Campbell River began to take over as the resource hub for the area when roads on Vancouver Island improved after World War I and a major fire in 1925, which swept down the middle of Quadra burning 20,000 hectares (50,000 acres) of timber and 11 farms, led to a decline in the island population. A new era in the island's fortunes started with the introduction of a car ferry service in 1960.

Many islanders develop a love-hate relationship with the ferry. It can be a brief pause before a busy trip to town, a social time to catch up with neighbours, or hurry up and wait. In the winter, fierce winds occasionally cause cancellations because it is too rough to dock at the Campbell River terminal, so prudent travellers leave a day early if they have travel connections. In the summer, ferry overloads are common, especially on holiday weekends. The transition from a resource-based economy, logging and commercial fishing, to tourism is a double-edged sword. Many islanders sigh with relief when the tourists leave and kids go back to school and the ferry line-ups return to normal.

Aerial view over Quadra looking up past Rebecca Spit toward Hoskyn Channel.

Above: A glimpse of a totem pole at Cape Mudge.

Right: During the 1930s handliners would build rowboats out of beach wood and live in driftwood shacks at Cape Mudge.

Campbell River to Quadra Ferry

BC Ferries' MV *Powell River Queen* shuttles back and forth across Discovery Passage like a water strider. Four omni-directional propulsion units, positioned on each corner of the vessel, allow maximum manoeuvrability. Onboard is a crew of seven: captain, mate, chief engineer, third engineer and three deckhands. Esther Allen, who grew up on Quadra and became BC Ferries' first woman skipper, is often on the bridge.

The MV Powell River Queen *unloading at Quathiaski Cove after the ten-minute run from Campbell River.*

Allen glances at the closed circuit deck display to make sure everything is ready for departure, checks with the deck crew for an "all clear," then starts to manoeuvre the ferry away from the dock. Over the radio she relays that she has 51 under-height vehicles and 128 passengers on board.

Winter is the most challenging time to command the ferry because seasonal storms bring fierce winds, driving rain and confused seas every three or four days. When there is a big swell the crew uses all four engines to hold the ferry against the berth for loading. If the storm is serious, they will wait on the more protected Quadra side until things calm down.

The engineer comes up on the bridge and I comment on the cleanliness of his overalls. "I'll tell you a little story. When my coveralls are dirty, you better be worried."

Every trip is different. In Discovery Passage tidal currents are quite strong and there are often counter-currents running along the shoreline. The captain must make constant course adjustments to allow for the ever-changing currents. Back in the 1980s and early '90s, when there were shoals of guide boats chasing salmon out in Discovery Passage, the crew once had to deploy a fire hose to clear a way through. Another time the ferry had to wait out in the Passage because an inebriated traveller decided to go for a swim at the Campbell River Terminal. Occasionally the crew will muster in the middle of the night to carry the ambulance across on an emergency run to Campbell River.

Quathiaski Cove

Mike King and Lewis Casey were logging in Quathiaski (which means "island in the mouth") Cove in the 1890s. Their logging camp had a wharf and a small store where islanders bought basics and mailed letters. When the logging camp closed down in 1893, Robert Hall took over the camp store and opened Quadra's first official post office. The Pidcock brothers opened a cannery on the shores of Quathiaski Cove in 1904. First Nation villagers from the We Wai Kai Reserve, just south of the cove, caught chinook and coho salmon with handlines from dugout canoes and sold them to the cannery. Many Cape Mudge women, who had experience working in canneries up and down the coast, were hired seasonally until the cannery was destroyed by fire in 1941. Fisheries regulations prohibited First Nations from running seine boats until 1922; however, by the 1950s, Quathiaski Cove was home port for a large fleet of seine boats, many of them run by crews from Cape Mudge village. With the drastically reduced fishing time allowed these days, several of the remaining seine boats transport farmed salmon to cover expenses.

Cape Mudge Village

At their peak the Laichwiltach numbered between four and ten thousand and Cape Mudge was one of their main villages. In his book *Assu of Cape Mudge*, Harry Assu told co-author Joy Inglis that after the flu epidemic in 1918, there were only 96 people remaining in the village. Since that time the village has rebounded and prospered through logging and fishing. The band made enough profit from logging its other reserve located near Rebecca Spit in the 1920s to tear down the last of the big houses and replace them with modern houses serviced by a central water system and one of the first electric plants in the area.

Harry Assu's grandson Frank Assu gives several reasons why his village has survived and prospered in *Lekwiltok Anthology: A collection of essays about the We Wai Kai People of Cape Mudge*. Assu recognizes that trading surplus food items such as salmon gave the We Wai Kai the necessary commercial experience to deal with white fur traders who arrived on the west coast looking for sea-otter skins. In addition, his people used skills learned over thousands of years to become top-producing fishboat skippers. From the 1930s until about the 1980s three-quarters of the villagers were employed in commercial fishing. These days employment in the seine fishing fleet has dropped to a third of what it was in the glory days although the band has diversified and continues to prosper. Statistically the We Wai Kai are almost a mirror image of the Wei Wai Kum, with a few slight differences. Population as of the 2006 census was 383, of whom 325 were registered Indians. Band members own 130 dwellings, most of which were more than twenty years old. Four percent speak Kwakwala at home; 27 percent have high school graduation and 4 percent have university degrees.

Nuyumbalees Cultural Centre

A statute outlawing the potlatch ceremony was passed in 1884 by the federal government, which saw it as key to a primitive belief system that was preventing Native people from adapting to modern society. The law was not strictly enforced until 1922 when 29 First Nations people were arrested after a potlatch that was held at the north end of Vancouver Island. Seventeen participants were sentenced to prison but were

Top left: A pole at the Cape Mudge reserve on Quadra Island.

Above: Ancient petroglyphs can be seen at low tide in Cape Mudge and near the Nuyumbalees Cultural Centre, where a few rocks have been moved for safekeeping.

offered a reprieve by the Indian agent if they forfeited all their masks and dance regalia and swore to give up potlatching. The masks and headgear were sent to Ottawa for safe-keeping but some articles were sold to collectors. After the potlatch prohibition was lifted in 1951, a long lobbying was undertaken to get the cultural treasures returned and the Nuyumbalees Cultural Centre was built to receive them. In 1979 there was a feast with 1,500 pounds of fire-roasted salmon to celebrate the opening of the Cultural Centre and repatriation of the potlatch regalia.

Next to the centre, the Kwi Kwi Gillas Cultural Education Centre is being developed for carving and dance programs. On May 13, 2007, Ah-Wah-qwa-dzas ("a place to relax and tell stories") was dedicated. Totems carved by local artists surround a fire pit designed for traditional salmon barbecue demonstrations.

Not far from the Cultural Centre is the Quadra United Church. Villagers built the small white church in 1931 with the proceeds from a successful fishing season and dedicated it to missionary R.J. Walker. In 1984 there was a special opening of the newly renovated church. A huge yellow cedar carving of a salmon behind the altar had been created by Haida carvers Bill Reid and Jim Hart. The stained glass window depicting a fishboat on the waves was done by island resident Russ Fuoco.

Today visitors can catch some of the flavour of We Wai Kai culture at the Tsa-kwa-Luten Lodge, which is located close to the old village site at the top of the bluffs. Opened by the We Wai Kai in 1991, the main lodge offers overnight accommodation and dining in a big house atmosphere with massive cedar posts, wall paintings by First Nation artist Mark Henderson and spectacular vistas down the Strait of Georgia. The remains of an old steam donkey that was used for logging reserve lands sits just north of the lodge. On the beach below the lodge there are 54 petroglyphs, rock art carvings in boulders, which are best seen at low tide.

Above: Welcome poles at Nuyumbalees Cultural Centre.

Right: Interior of the Nuyumbalees Cultural Centre on the Cape Mudge Reserve. This fascinating museum was built to display potlatch regalia repatriated to the band.

Cape Mudge Lighthouse

When the Cape Mudge Lighthouse was built in 1898 just in time to light the way for the flotilla of vessels heading north for the Yukon Gold Rush, it was a squat wooden building with the light in a raised cupola. The current 17.5-metre (58-foot) concrete tower was built at a later date. The first lightkeepers, John and Annie Davidson, lit a coal-oil light every night and hand-cranked a warning horn during foggy spells. Jim Abram, Quadra's director to the Strathcona Regional District, worked at the lighthouse for 18 years. During that time the government had been trying to automate and de-staff lights to save money and Abram lobbied hard over the years, citing the ability of lightkeepers to render emergency assistance to mariners and relay on-the-spot weather reports to floatplane pilots as invaluable services. Sadly, at time of writing the Coast Guard had once again placed Cape Mudge on the block for de-staffing.

Early Logging and Mining on Quadra Island

As on other parts of the coast, the first loggers on Quadra worked alone, using hand tools to drop easily accessible trees into the water. Small logging companies started using slow-paced but strong oxen to haul logs out of the woods. Oxen were replaced by horses, which were faster. In 1890 Hugh Grant pioneered float camps, large timber rafts with housing for both loggers and oxen, to cut hard-to-access areas like Granite Point on the north end of the island. The largest company working on Quadra Island was the venerable Hastings Mill Company of Vancouver, which started railway logging in Granite Bay with "Old Curly," an ancient locomotive used in construction of the CPR and Panama Canal, now on display at the Burnaby Heritage Village. By 1908 Hastings had five steam donkeys yarding timber out of the woods to the rail tracks. About this time the company also financed the Lucky Jim Gold Mine, as they could use their rail

The first Cape Mudge Lighthouse, a squat wooden building, was completed in 1898 in time for the Klondike gold rush. Today's lighthouse is a 17.5-metre concrete tower.

tracks to ship out the ore. The large steel flywheel can still be seen at the old mine site just off Granite Bay Road. Truck logging took over from the railways after World War II and in recent years locally owned small-scale woodlots have replaced the large corporate logging operations.

Lucky Jim Mine, Granite Bay, Quadra Island, 1908–1913. Noble collection, Museum of Campbell River 20191-32

The Changing Face of Quathiaski Cove

Bill O'Connor is a Quadra Island old-timer who logged all over the island. He bought land on Quadra in 1965, and in between logging and running a sawmill built the first commercial buildings in the Quathiaski Cove Plaza. Over the years O'Connor figures he and his wife Freda owned about 27 pieces of island property that they mostly sold to locals. He had to finance some of the sales, but found islanders always paid him back.

Outside his shop there is a Raven Lumber sign. The island was fairly polarized when Campbell River-based Raven decided to log its forest lands in the middle of the island. "Why not?" says O'Connor, who claims that Quadra has the best second-growth fir in the world due to its climate and soil. He views trees dispassionately as a crop: "One-hundred-year-old wood, time to log it, grow it again."

O'Connor donated land for the Seniors' Housing Project, which is planning to build small low-cost rental units in Quathiaski Cove. In 2010 the regional district hired David Rousseau, a planner from neighbouring Cortes Island, to hold a series of public meetings to discuss a multi-generational, pedestrian-friendly, green-village concept for the cove. One quote that came out of the public meetings—"The Cove initiative is a big idea that needs to behave like a small idea in order to be acceptable for Quadra"—sums up island life perfectly.

Quadra Arts

Painters, potters and writers are drawn to islands for inspiration and the slower pace of life. "Swinging from trapeze to trapeze," however, is how one writer describes the challenge of making a living in the arts. A local poet gathers both inspiration and money deckhanding during prawn and salmon season. The arts alliance published an artists' directory and the annual Quadra Studio Tour is a highlight for many visitors who come to browse through more than twenty studios all over the island.

Shane Philip: Quadra Musician

Making a living playing a didgeridoo seems a stretch for an ex-high school teacher and former kayak guide, but Shane Philip exudes an air of calm happiness about the direction his life is taking. He and his partner have a young child and he has launched his third CD since taking up music full-time.

Shane was born in Ottawa and after university migrated west to teach school in Smithers, BC. One day he visited Quadra and fell in love with the island lifestyle. He would spend summers working as a kayak guide for a local tour company and winters teaching in Smithers. A chance meeting with a didgeridoo player from Cortes Island led Shane to take up the Australian wind instrument. He takes his distinctive sound on tour to the summer festivals around BC and has built up a loyal following. After leaving teaching for life as a musician, he says he makes a comparable living, is happier and has a better home life.

Shane Philip performing. Michael Desjardins photo

Hilary Stewart: Quadra Island Author

Hilary Stewart grew up on St. Lucia, a small island in the Caribbean about two-thirds the size of Quadra and is renowned for her books on northwestern First Nation culture such as *Cedar*. Her book *On Island Time* is a more personal look at life on Quadra. She bought land and asked local architect Rob Wood to design a house, but for eight years she was too busy researching and writing books to live on Quadra.

Stewart writes about the joys of island life: violet green swallows taking up residence in her nest boxes, tree frogs that appear in the oddest places, native plants that can be turned into jams and teas; even slugs are celebrated in her writing. With her anthropologist friend Joy Inglis she explores petroglyphs, the rock art depictions of the spirit world created by First Nations artists. Her sketches of the plant life on Mitlenatch Island—tiger lily, prickly pear cactus, harvest brodiaea and woolly sunflower—lighten the pages. My favourite memory of Stewart took place during a school lecture. The kids watched in awe as she took off her shoes and socks to demonstrate how First Nations weavers used their toes to hold cedar twigs when making fishing lines.

Hilary Stewart enjoying the view from the deck of the *Aurora Explorer*.
Marcia Wolter photo

The Coffee Crowds

There's a saying on the "Rock," as the Quadrapods sometimes call it, that "Quadra is a great place to live, hard place to make a living," meaning that a large number of people commute to jobs in Campbell River or work off-island in logging camps and fish farms. With the advent of the internet there is a new dynamic. A look at two island coffee haunts bears this out. It's local business with concepts drawn on the backs of napkins that matter for the ten o'clock Quathiaski Cove crowd at the Lovin' Oven. Up the road at Café Aroma people are hunched over their laptops, posting resumés and checking stocks.

Shane Mallis has owned Aroma for the last couple of years. In the winter people gravitate to the tables by the heater and in the summer the outdoor tables usually have a chess game in progress. Throughout the day locals drop by for coffee, tea, snacks and gossip. When there is a power outage, the Cove often still has power, so people come in to warm up with a coffee, listen to local CDs and check their email. Local artists show their work on the walls and local musicians play in the evenings.

When the Power Fails

Another thing that the winds and rains bring is frequent power outages, which can last from hours to almost a week when wind and wet snow topples trees onto the power lines. Certain parts of Quathiaski Cove will have power while the rest of the island relies on generators, propane lights and flashlights. Islanders, hearing of an approaching storm, will fill bathtubs and water containers as many homes rely on electric pumps to bring water up from their wells. A must-have is a corded phone as the convenient portable phone won't work when the power goes out. Another island survival technique is having an uninterrupted power supply for computer systems. Laptops have battery backup but a blip in power with a desktop can be disastrous. Many homes now have a backup generator, insurance against losing the contents of their freezers.

Above: The spa facility at April Point Resort on Quadra Island.

Right: The April Point Resort, started by the Peterson family as an upscale fishing lodge in the late 1940s, is now owned by the Oak Bay Marine Group.

April Point Lodge

From the dining room at April Point Lodge there is a spectacular view of mountainous cruise ships parading down Discovery Passage. The Peterson family bought the property by the south entrance to Gowlland Harbour in 1948 and over the years built up a fishing lodge that attracted customers from around the world. Many would base their yachts in the marina tucked at the head of the bay. After Mr. Peterson's death in the 1970s, his sons and wife continued to run the resort, hosting celebs like Bob Hope and John Wayne, who were avid salmon fishermen. In 1998, the Petersons sold the property to the Oak Bay Marine Group, who undertook extensive renovations. In 2005 the Aveda Spa was added, offering an assortment of health and beauty treatments.

Salmon Enhancement

Part of island life is the increase in wind and rain when the leaves turn and the geese fly south in fall. The storms bring rain, which raises water levels in the creeks, allowing salmon to ascend and spawn. Past logging practices, such as damming creeks so that they could be used to float logs down to the ocean, greatly affected the salmon runs by blocking passage. The Quadra Island Salmon Enhancement Society has been trying to restore those runs by adding spawning gravel and restoring natural cover to the streams. The QISES celebrated its 30th anniversary in 2010. Today, twenty to thirty volunteers monitor five island streams for spawning activity and the good news is that the salmon are slowly returning to the streams.

Island Policing

Henry Jones, the first police constable in the Discovery Islands, began patrols from Powell River to the Thurlow Islands in 1902. Ten years later a police station, with jail cells and a courthouse, was built in Quathiaski Cove.

Postings to Quadra's RCMP four-person detachment, which also polices neighbouring Cortes Island, are normally three years and Sergeant Craig Peterson has completed three tours on Quadra. In his first tour of duty, Peterson dealt mostly with minor property crimes such as the burglar who would visit the islands breaking into holiday cottages. The Quadra detachment is also responsible for neighbouring Cortes Island, which they access with a police boat, but the sergeant says, "Most people on Cortes deal with situations themselves, as they know it will take some time for the police to arrive."

A salmon at the end of its journey.

When Peterson and his family arrived in 1998 the Quadra school had more than two hundred pupils, a principal and vice-principal. Now there are fewer than a hundred enrolled as the island population ages and rising land prices make it difficult for young families to live here.

Part of his job is marijuana patrols in the fall harvest season. This form of tax-free horticulture has allowed some islanders to supplement their income but urban indoor marijuana grow operations have generally taken over from outdoor pot growing. One island story involves a summer resident who opened his garage to find that pot growers had used it for a warehouse to store fertilizer stolen from the local building supply store.

Peterson has enjoyed his time on the island; however, his pet peeve is summer visitors who drink openly in public, figuring that this is "just Quadra."

Rebecca Spit

Many islanders consider Rebecca Spit Provincial Park to be the heart of Quadra. Located on the opposite side of Quadra from Campbell River, the distant snow-capped Coast Mountain Range on the mainland forms a backdrop to neighbouring Cortes and Marina islands. The low-lying spit has a long, wide, sandy beach curving around a

Right: Hikers atop Chinese Mountain take in the view overlooking Hyacinthe Bay, Heriot Bay and Rebecca Spit.

Below: A popular walking trail goes out to the tip of Rebecca Spit.

Bottom: The grade 3 class from Quadra Elementary performing the traditional Maypole dance during May Day. Ian Douglas photo

protected anchorage. Any time of the year is great for walking the trail to the tip of the spit and on warm summer evenings islanders take their barbecues down to the picnic area so the parents can socialize while the kids jump and splash in the ocean. Building driftwood forts is so much fun that it has become one of the events at the annual May Day festivities.

May Day has been held at Rebecca Spit for more than a century. An opening parade with the Campbell River Legion Bagpipe Band and hand-decorated floats is one of the highlights of the May Day celebrations. There is a May Queen chosen from the graduating class on Quadra, a maypole dance, a grease pole with money at the top, three-legged races for the kids, various food tents and a fiercely contested sailboat race.

The We Wai Kai operate a 146-site public campground on their reserve by the spit. They are also running a deep-water scallop farm in the coastal waters south of the reserve.

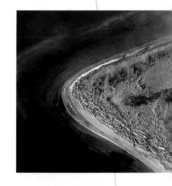

The tip of Rebecca Spit is reduced to a simple design of soft undulating curves.

Building a Community Centre

The Quadra Island Community Centre is located midway between Heriot Bay and Quathiaski Cove. Cesar Caflisch designed the post-and-beam hall that was started in 1983 and completed to lockup stage two years later. It has been a work in progress ever since and new facilities are added as the island grows. Community centre coordinator Sandy Spearing organizes the annual May Day celebration as well as community events such as dances and workshops. She came to Quadra in 1973 as part of the back-to-the-land movement. "We were looking for a place to find a home. We were 23-year-olds and wanted to have a kid, wanted to find a place where we could nest."

In the beginning regular fundraiser dances were held to finance completion of the building. "I remember one of the early dances. We used to have great dances because everybody was 30 and, before we were all conscious about drinking and driving, the dances were huge and wild." "Gumboot helicopters" was a phrase coined for whirling islanders in long skirts and patchouli oil. The goal of one particular dance was to raise money to put tile on the cement floor because what they didn't foresee was what happens when two hundred people dance on cement. "After a couple of hours we were in a cloud of cement dust."

Sandy was constantly fundraising until islanders voted in 1991 to support the community centre with their property taxes. She sees Quadra Island as a series of little communities, with the community centre as neutral ground where these smaller groups can interact.

One of the events that invites interaction is the community lunch that began about four or five years ago. Volunteers come in once a week to cook a lunch that draws everyone from the very rich to people who live on the margins. "The beauty of this place," says Sandy, "is that people volunteer, and once you volunteer, you own it. People come in and spend a couple hours doing the dishes at the community kitchen or something. And you can see that they really start taking part, they start owning what's happening, and that's the miracle of this place, because it's truly the community."

Camp Homewood

Generations of island kids have gone to summer camp at Camp Homewood on Gowlland Harbour. Alf and Margaret Bayne cruised the coast in their 11-metre (36-foot) mission boat holding Bible camps for the Pacific Coast Children's Mission until they decided to become land-based. In 1948 the Pacific Coast Children's Mission bought Homewood Farm on the waterfront in Gowlland Harbour, just north of Quathiaski Cove. Over the years a wharf and buildings were added to the original property and today there is an active summer program for kids that includes horseback riding, sailing lessons and camping on Main Lake on the north end of the island.

Sam Whittingham: the Fastest Man on Two Wheels

Quadra native Sam Whittingham builds custom bikes and is world-renowned as the first person to break the deciMach speed record: one-tenth the speed of sound (132 km/h). Sam's quiet and unassuming character hides the fact that his 5-foot 7-inch body is a deadly effective pedalling machine. Riding a recumbent bike with a carbon-fibre shell at the 2008 annual World Human Powered Speed Challenge in Battle Mountain in Nevada, Sam reached 132.5 km/h (82 mph) and claimed the $26,000 prize.

After studying design at the University of Victoria and working in a bike shop, Sam started his company, Naked Bicycles and Design, in 1997. In his wood-heated shop there is a sandblasting cabinet, painting room, a drill press and a TIG welder. Completed wheels hang from the ceiling. Sam often uses wood rims that are only made in Italy. He uses mostly steel for frames but is experimenting with stainless steel and titanium. Emmy, as his jig is nicknamed, holds the frame together as it is finely fitted and welded.

A custom bike takes six months from concept to delivery and Sam builds about sixty bikes a year. At last count he was offering 18 base models to choose from. Price ranges from $2,700 up to $12,000 with the average around $3,500 to $4,000. His main market is people who have ridden for forty years and now want something really special. He built a blue and red Superman model for the producer on *Smallville*, a popular TV show about the superhero. Sam says by the time he is finished a bike for a client it feels

Sam Whittingham, the fastest man on two wheels at 132.5 km/h (82 mph), in his bike-building shop on Quadra.

Quadra is covered with a wide variety of bike trails, including the Morte Lake circuit, which is fast becoming a favourite destination for riders.

less like a business relationship and more like a friendship. People often come for a fitting and many people make the trip to Quadra to pick up their finished bike. Sam's won many awards at the Handmade Bike Show in the US and the pièce de résistance was selling an award-winning bike to Tour-de-France superstar Lance Armstrong.

Keeping it Local: The Old Farm Community Garden

Fei and Milton Wong, owners of the Taku Resort in Drew Harbour, are leasing an acre of land on their farm south of Heriot Bay for a dollar per year so that islanders can grow their own food in a community garden. The idea for the garden came from sustainability workshops that led to the formation of a local food directory and a garden-sharing program. A food registry was set up to distribute excess fruit from island gardeners and then the idea for a community garden bloomed. A public meeting was held in 2009 to see if there was interest for the concept and the project took off. Funding for the community garden came from different sources and many islanders volunteered their time preparing the 35 plots. Although most of the plots are tended by individual households, the island food bank, community kitchen, school and Quadra Children's Centre have plots tended by volunteers.

The Heriot Bay Inn

The Heriot Bay Inn has been a community watering hole and gathering place for more than a century. Hosea Bull was an island entrepreneur who realized that the loggers and miners who worked on the island wouldn't mind paying for the occasional libation. The problem was, loggers and miners mixed like oil and water socially. Island historian Jeanette Taylor recounts epic battles in the bar. On one memorable occasion the combatants fought until they were exhausted, slept, and then started again when they woke up.

The present building dates from the early 1920s but the original steamship wharf

The Heriot Bay Inn on Quadra Island is a well-known destination for boaters and island residents alike.

From the chairs in front of the Heriot Bay Inn you can watch people preparing for their first kayak trip, sailboats pulling into the marina and prawn boats delivering their catch at the government dock.

in front of the hotel has been replaced by a marina, gas dock and adventure centre. The current owners of the HBI are a group of islanders who have put a lot of creative energy into upgrading the facilities. There is an attractive gift shop, and the dining room often has folk nights during the winter and jazz on summer weekends, when boaters not moored at the marina will dinghy over from Rebecca Spit to have dinner on the deck.

Quadra Architecture

Due to the lack of a building code on Quadra there is an island aesthetic that has resulted in many unique and unusual designs. The Tulip House has a freeform tower covered in cedar shakes, the Onion House is a cedar shake dome and one house has a car in the living room.

Skid homes, basic one-storey cabins built on foundations of pointed logs, were used extensively in the early days of logging as they could be dragged along when the action moved down the beach. Many of those skid homes were retired from logging and turned into beachfront homesteads.

In later years mobile homes were a quick and inexpensive housing alternative on Quadra Island. They would grow organically with the addition of a metal roof to form a porch and a woodshed tacked on the back. Gradually additional rooms would grow around the original home and it would be time to remove the mobile unit and replace it with proper frame construction.

Now, with wealthy retirees building large homes, there is employment for the island contractors but with the rise in land prices locals are finding it harder and harder to buy land of their own. On many of the islands wealthy landowners have to do their own cleaning and yard maintenance as the supply of local labour moves off-island to more affordable areas.

Kayaks to Go

Kayak tourism has become a significant business on Quadra due to sheltered local waters that are perfect for beginners. Five operators offer day trips and multi-day trips. One of the first, Spirit of the West Adventures, started offering day trips from

A novice paddler looks a little apprehensive as a brooding sky develops at the onset of a kayaking adventure.

Rebecca Spit in 1997 and by its third year had multi-day trips heading to Johnstone Strait where the highlight is the chance to paddle with orcas.

The kayak companies hire quite a few graduates of the adventure tourism course at North Island College in Campbell River and many of the kayak guides end up settling on Quadra.

Walcan Seafood

Open 12 months of the year, Walcan Seafood is a processing company located in Discovery Passage, just south of Seymour Narrows. Walcan employs 135 workers, half of whom live on Quadra while the other half commute from Campbell River. Bill Pirie,

Jim Lornie and Norm Brown started Walcan in 1974 to process sport-caught salmon and freeze herring into packages for sportfish bait. In later years the owners expanded and modernized the production lines to process farmed salmon raised in local waters, herring roe on kelp, prawns, shellfish and wild salmon.

Mid-March to April is roe-on-kelp season on the west coast. Herring lay eggs on kelp blades and the eggs are sorted, graded and packed in brine before being shipped to Japan, where it is a prized delicacy. Prawn season is May and June with half of the product being flown from the fishing grounds to the plant to preserve the quality while the rest is frozen on the boats at sea. Most of the prawns go into the Japanese sushi market.

Being flexible is a necessary economic strategy to keep the plant running. Walcan processes herring for sportfishing bait between November and March. There is a developing pilchard fishery in the fall. Pilchards, a type of sardine, are packed for food and longline bait. Commercially caught salmon are processed as fresh, frozen and value-added. Recently, Walcan started cleaning and packaging locally grown Gallo mussels. Farmed salmon is processed year-round, some delivered by local fish packers and some trucked in from the west coast of Vancouver Island. Once in the plant the fish are cleaned by hand, sent through an automated weigh station that sorts them by size then finally down into the boxing station where they are packed in Styrofoam containers. Shipped by truck and by air, in most cases the fish are on store shelves within 24 hours.

Atlantic salmon are gutted with heads on at the Walcan Seafood processing plant on Quadra Island in preparation for distribution.

Island Memorials

Brian Stevenson showed up on Quadra in the early '70s with a parrot on his shoulder and spent the next thirty years working as a commercial diver and oyster farmer. He died when his oyster skiff went down in bad weather off Rebecca Spit in December 2008. His crew member Troy Bouchard survived several hours in the frigid water and a night ashore on a nearby island. The Coast Guard and islanders started searching when Stevenson and Bouchard were reported overdue and Bouchard was found cold but alive early the next morning. Stevenson was a popular character and his memorial service/wake at the Heriot Bay Inn was standing room only and was still going at five the next morning.

Several months later a carving of a large wooden oyster was bolted into place by the Heriot Bay boat ramp and dedicated to Stevenson. The carver, Vinay Chafekar, said that even though he hadn't known Stevenson personally, he was struck by the community effort involved in the search. Chafekar had first visited Quadra in 1984 on a boating holiday. When it came time to retire from university life, he was looking for a vibrant and caring community so he moved to Quadra.

Not far from where the oyster skiff foundered there is a memorial bench overlooking the ocean, this one dedicated to five passengers who went down on a Beaver floatplane after taking off from Campbell River on February 28, 2005. Both memorials are reminders of how much the islanders' lives still depend on keeping peace with the elements.

Vinay Chafekar created this memorial to local oyster farmer Brian Stevenson who was lost off Rebecca Spit in 2008. Ian Douglas photo

3

Cortes Island

Preceding pages: T'ai Li Lodge on Cortes Island provides a choice seat for a spectacular predawn view.

"It begins with water. I grew up beside the ocean, to a constant water song that runs so deeply it mostly remains subterranean to the conscious awareness of those of us who are rocked by that vast cradle. An island is created by water and surrounded by water, and is entirely enveloped by a horizon line. It is, for me, defined by its place between the sea and the sky."

—*Brigid Weiler,* Islands in the Salish Sea: A Community Atlas *(2005)*

Although only slightly smaller than Quadra, Cortes Island has a totally different character. Cortes, officially named for the conqueror of Mexico by the Spanish explorers Galiano and Valdes, has been called the Island of Driveways.

Below: Cortes Island attracts the individual seeking a slower pace and alternative lifestyle, including this young woman who lives on her float house and greets each day with yoga and meditation.

Bottom right: All kinds of watercraft visit the islands in the summer.

There seems to be no central gathering place for the one thousand inhabitants (except perhaps the Friday market at Manson's Hall), only leafy lanes leading into the forest. Two ferry rides—the 10-minute crossing of Discovery Passage from Campbell River to Quathiaski Cove, the drive across Quadra and the 45-minute trip from Heriot Bay on the east side of Quadra Island to Whaletown on the southwest corner of Cortes—slow the pace of life compared to the more easily accessible commuter islands like Quadra or Bowen. With such an investment in time and money, some Cortesians, as locals are known, may go months between off-island trips.

Several First Nation Salishan-speakers, known collectively as Mainland Comox, shared the resources of Cortes. For thousands of years Natives hunted deer and seal, fished for salmon and cod and dug clams on this island blessed with numerous bays. In Gorge Harbour at low tide there are remnants of clam gardens, rock terraces built up to improve the shellfish habitat. The Sliammon First Nation from the Desolation Sound area spent part of the year fishing for chum salmon at Paukeanam ("place where the maple leaves turn brown") on the south end of the island. The Klahoose, who hunted and fished in the area and spent their winters in villages in Toba Inlet, had two reserves set aside for them in Squirrel Cove on the northeast coast in 1888. They moved to Squirrel Cove from Toba in 1896 at the urging of Oblate missionaries after severe flooding at their winter village.

The massive stands of Douglas fir on Cortes drew loggers to the area in the late 1880s. Michael Manson, one of the island pioneers who started a trading post at Clytosin, later named Mansons Landing, registered a pre-emption at Gunflint Lake in 1887, the first on Cortes. Safe harbours shaped much of the island's development. Steamer docks at Whaletown, Mansons Landing, Cortes Bay and Squirrel Cove were the main access points to the island until the regular steamer service ended in the 1950s.

Ferry service started in 1969 when the population was around four hundred and only a year before the island was hooked up to the electrical grid. Now the island population almost doubles in the summer. On long weekends ferry overloads can be expected and islanders will often park a car in the line-up overnight to be assured of a spot in the morning.

Islanders can also go to town on the Cortes Connection, a minibus that heads to

Far left: Treasures are guaranteed when beachcombing along Cortes's spectacular coastline.

Left: Young woman displays a 10-metre diet, fresh salad from the Hollyhock garden.

Below: Lifestyle at T'ai Li Lodge on Cortes Island.

Above: Salmon baked over a fire using the traditional First Nations method.

Right: Mainland Comox First Nations shared the resources of Cortes for thousands of years. Nowadays oyster growers raise shellfish on this island blessed with bays.

A little passenger enjoying her ferry ride to Cortes.

Campbell River on the morning ferry and returns in the evening. The health centre on Cortes has an arrangement with the Quadra pharmacy so prescriptions can be phoned in and placed on the ferry. Orders for building materials can be placed with Quadra Builders as they bring over a delivery truck most days.

The ferry ride is a relaxing trip in the summer, a time when friends and neighbours catch up on island goings-on. The ferry bulletin board is an eclectic mix of island events and articles for sale. One summer a humpback whale occasionally breached alongside the ferry to the delight of passengers and crew. A winter ride can be a whole different experience because of the rough weather. It is up to ferry skippers to cancel or delay a run when they judge conditions too rough.

Whaletown

Whaletown was named for the whaling station that operated in the bay for a year in 1869. Crew of the schooner *Kate,* working for the Dawson Whaling Company of Victoria, killed 14 whales that were rendered down to 150 barrels of oil. The whalers moved on but the huge stands of Douglas fir attracted Moses Ireland, a logger and timber-cruiser who starting logging at the old whale works and later built a hotel on Subtle Island off the southwest corner of Cortes.

Cortes Post Office

In 1894 William Drinkwater and Lawrence Rose opened a small store and post office in their home in Whaletown. The post office was moved in 1940 to the tiny building still in use adjacent to the Whaletown dock. Visitors can stop to mail a letter postmarked with the oldest postal cancel stamp in continuous use in Canada.

Left: *Whaletown Whimsy* by Cortes artist **Dianne Bersea.** Dianne Bersea CSPWC AFCA photo

Below: Protected harbours like Whaletown make cruising around Cortes Island a dream.

People come from near and far to visit Dr. Dale Anderson, the floating dentist.

The Floating Dentist

Cortes has the distinction of being served by the coast's only floating dentist. Dr. Dale Anderson originally operated his practice from his sailboat after he returned from a trip to Tahiti. He tied up his current practice—a float house 12 metres long by 9 metres wide (40 by 30 feet)—in Whaletown in 1999. From the dentist's chair you can watch the hustle and bustle of daily dock life. In addition to his regular Cortes patients, outer islanders boat to his office and Quadra patients come as foot passengers on the ferry.

Gilean Douglas

Often called a Canadian Thoreau, Gilean Douglas was born in Toronto in 1900. She travelled extensively as a reporter and freelanced for a wide variety of publications. When her nature writing was rejected by a male editor she began to write under the male pen name of Grant Madison. *River for My Sidewalk* (1953), a book about her experiences living in a cabin in the Cascade Mountains near Kamloops, was published under her male alias. After her mountain cabin burned down she bought the abandoned 57-hectare (140-acre) John Pool homestead at Channel Rock in Uganda Passage between Cortes and Marina islands. She describes her arrival at Channel Rock and life on Cortes in *The Protected Place*, published in 1979 under her own byline. Douglas was active in the Cortes Women's Institute, an educational organization founded in 1897 to help rural women learn home-making skills and promote community health projects. She was an official weather observer and served both as a regional director and on the environmental committee dealing with conservation issues. She wrote a column for the *Victoria Times Colonist* for 31 years called "Nature Rambles." Douglas passed away surrounded by friends in her 93rd year and her small home on Channel Rock looking toward Shark Spit is now run as an educational retreat.

Above: Gilean Douglas was a nature writer who became a weather observer and regional director when she moved to Cortes. Cortes Island Museum and Archives Society photo

Right: Cortes Seniors visit Gilean Douglas' Channel Rock house which is now run as an educational retreat. Ester Strijbos photo

Theatre on Cortes

Each year Linnaea, the island's alternative school, puts on theatrical productions at the Gorge Community Hall, located just up from the old government wharf in Gorge Harbour. Donna Bracewell, principal for twenty years, said that of all the things she'd done with the kids, the theatrical productions were the best. She admitted each new production was a lot of work but they were invaluable for teaching students about teamwork, tolerance and a sense of community. "And acting is an incredible self-esteem builder."

King Arthur at Gorge Hall

Tickets go quickly for the annual Linnaea School production. Gorge Hall, built in 1933 on land donated by local homesteader George Beattie, has the feel of a favourite sweater, comfortable and a little frayed around the edges from decades of dances and community celebrations. When the Linnaea students presented *The Hobbit* last year, the entrance to the hall was decorated with branches to look like a hobbit hole. Organic snacks and buffalo kabobs with blackberry pie for dessert are offered at the side of the hall and comfy armchairs in the front row are labelled "Seniors Only." As proud parents in patchwork jackets and black jeans fill the seats, a hint of patchouli oil floats in the air. This year, Donna Bracewell re-tuned the Arthurian legend to include strong female roles, elaborate costumes and well-choreographed battle scenes. It had been raining before the play started but during intermission the sun came out and parents took off their kids' shoes so they could play in the mud. The highlight of the second act was the dancing dragon. Original soundtracks from the Linnaea productions, as well as the school play kits, are available on the internet.

Gorge Harbour Resort

Gorge Harbour is a large bay on the southwest side of the island that has a narrow entrance guarded by a high cliff that was used by First Nations as a defensive position. There are pictographs (rock paintings) on the cliff face and an old village site on the opposite shore.

The Gorge Harbour Resort is built on the former Allen homestead in the northwest corner of the bay. The Allen brothers were among the first settlers on Cortes, and Charlie Allen partnered with a Chinese logging crew to clear his property in the early 1900s. The marina was started in 1968; the current owner, Dr. Richard Glickman, bought the resort in 2004. Glickman grew up cruising the BC coast in a variety of boats and became alarmed at the number of small marinas that were being closed to the public. Since 2004 the molecular biologist has been busy upgrading the facilities. In 2009 he put in an outdoor pool and during the summer season he and his wife Michelle have been hosting music nights and Friday night oyster fests with grower and seafood promoter Brent Petkau on the deck at the head of the docks.

Large pleasure boats tied up for the evening at the Gorge Harbour Resort on Cortes Island.

Cortes Seafood

Oyster grower Brent Petkau is passionate about seafood. "The best way to eat an oyster is definitely raw and naked… Just a beautiful oyster experience—delectable."

Oysters have a long history on Cortes. It was one of the few places to have beds of the rare native oyster, discovered in 1895 in Carrington Bay and Von Donop Inlet on

Above: The eclectic and passionate Brent Petkau, the "oyster man," is well known in food circles for his energy and love of the oyster.

Right: The annual OysterFest on Cortes includes a giant oyster contest as well as a seafood buffet, music and fun for the children.

the west side of the island. Japanese oysters were introduced to BC waters in 1912 and were first commercially harvested from Von Donop Inlet in 1938. By the 1980s large oyster co-operatives were growing shellfish on Cortes beaches and suspended from lines in Gorge Harbour. There is an ongoing debate between landowners and oyster farmers about aquaculture operations disturbing the tranquillity of the foreshore. What isn't up for debate is the gastronomic appeal of the end product. The annual spring OysterFest held in Squirrel Cove each May attracts scores of seafood aficionados. At the 2008 OysterFest 5,000 oysters, 109 kilograms (240 pounds) of clams, 34 litres (30 quarts) of prawn tails and 136 litres (30 gallons) of chowder were served to the crowd.

Linnaea School and Farm

Linnaea School was an alternative school for fifty island children located on a working organic farm at Gunflint Lake in the middle of the island. The Hansen family, the third generation of Manson relations to live on Cortes, started a summer camp for kids there in 1953 and Linnaea School opened in 1987.

Donna Bracewell was the principal for twenty years. When she came to Cortes with her six children, there were no paved roads, only party telephone lines and most of the parents worked in resource industries with just a few professionals living on the island.

Bracewell started with a one-room schoolhouse for kindergarten to grade 6 students in a Quonset hut and ten years later added a second classroom and a large community room, where all the students and staff meet every morning. "We had a whole group of kids that had been with us since kindergarten and they were going to graduate. The parents wanted us to keep their kids in the school so we expanded to grades 7 and 8. Two of the parents were builders and they helped build the addition."

Tuition was $3,200 per year with a strong scholarship program, and parents could trade construction work for tuition fees. Children came out of the Linnaea program with a strong connection to nature after spending time in the garden and looking after the farm animals. The teachers worked with the students on conflict resolution, tolerance and diversity in order to prepare them for high school. Because there is no high school on Cortes, children must go to Campbell River, and a lot of families move off-island when that time comes. Low enrollment closed the school in 2010.

The Linnaea Farm Ecological Gardening Program was started in 1987 by David Buckner. The residential eight-month-long program offers a thorough grounding in organic gardening and small-scale farming through a full growing season. Eleven students a year work and learn in the main garden, which has been in production for over a century. The farm is also the site of a potato co-op with 25 families, which has been ongoing for 21 years. Linnaea Farm provides the land, seed, equipment and organization. Co-op members, who pay a nominal yearly membership fee, work together to plant, hill, weed and harvest the crop.

Friends of Cortes Island

The small building behind the Manson's Community Hall is the Friends of Cortes Island (FOCI) office. FOCI is an environmental charity with about 300 members that monitors the health of the island foreshore, has a lending library of environmental books and audio-visuals, maintains the popular hiking trails in Kw'as Park and Carrington Bay Park and conducts alternative-energy workshops.

Cortes Island Museum

The Cortes Museum opened its doors in 1996 just up Beasley Road from the Manson's Community Hall. The building used to be the general store located down by the dock in Manson's Lagoon. Elmer and May Ellingsen, the son of a pioneer logger and Mike Manson's granddaughter, organized and paid for the move to the present location. The museum has an extensive collection of archival photos as well as displays covering First Nations, fishing, forestry and pioneer life on the island.

A participant is costumed for the Beltane pagan festival at Linnaea Alternative School.

Cortes Island Seniors Society

Island time means that projects sometimes take a little longer than anticipated. Back in 1987 property and building materials were donated to the Cortes Island Seniors Society so it could build affordable housing. The project was on hold until a government grant pushed things forward. The Cortes Island Seniors Society was justifiably proud when six housing units for seniors opened next to the health centre in June 2009.

Cortes Island Natural Food Co-op

Started in 2004, the Cortes Island Natural Food Co-op has grown to 550 member-families and in 2009 hit the million-dollar revenue mark. The aim of the co-op is to get islanders eating locally, whether it is through the co-op or buying directly from growers. In recent years 19 percent of the store's produce was locally grown. With yearly fees of only $30, members are encouraged to grow more food for local consumption, and to sell to the co-op so that less food has to be sourced off-island.

Manson's Community Hall

Manson's Hall on the corner of Beasley and Sutil roads is the island centre during Friday market days in the summer. People come to pick up their mail, cruise through the library offerings, check out the market and have lunch in the café in the hall.

The Cortes Island market is held inside and outside Manson's Hall. Painters display their latest canvases, troll-caught sockeye is sold by an island fisherman, weavers and silversmiths set up next to displays of mouth-watering baked goods. Several of the artists also exhibit their work at the artist co-op craft store near the general store in Squirrel Cove.

Cortes DJ

The Cortes Community Radio Station is also located in the Manson's Community Hall. A volunteer-run organization, it was started in 2005 to provide alternative programming with a community focus. Broadcasting 24/7, it has over 126 hours of live programming per week including interviews, documentaries and children's story time. Since all islands are subject to power outages, the control room has a bank of deep-cycle batteries as well as generator backup. Above the venerable turntable is a stern warning about the delicacy of tone-arm cartridges and a "Do not turn this knob" sign on the blinking control panel.

Greg Osoba is one of the dedicated DJs whose passionate and diverse musical interest makes the station so popular. Osoba had worked in radio newsrooms in Toronto, Edmonton and Vancouver and was looking for a break. He came up for a workshop at Hollyhock, the alternative learning centre on the south end of the island, and afterwards met a gardener who was looking for an assistant. That was February 1989. The island immediately felt like home, and twenty years slipped by. He switched jobs, from trail building to program catalogue production, and now is the marketing manager at Hollyhock.

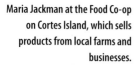

Greg Osoba came to Cortes for a workshop and twenty years slipped away . . .
Al Westnedge photo

Maria Jackman at the Food Co-op on Cortes Island, which sells products from local farms and businesses.

Dianne Bersea, Island Artist

Dianne Bersea is a Cortes artist who once had a day job designing and illustrating exhibitions for Parks Canada. Her latest works are a series of views of Squirrel Cove, T'ai Li Lodge and Gorge Harbour where she translates the landscape into a whimsical aerial view. She came to Hollyhock with another artist 14 years ago and stayed. When she moved to the island she did what locals call the "Cortes shuffle." She rented a house but had to move out and camp every summer when the owners came up. Eventually she and her partner Jodi Forster bought property close to Mansons where they set up a B&B with a studio in the backyard. Dianne holds art retreats and watercolour workshops while Jody carves and helps run the B&B.

Hollyhock

Founded in 1982, Hollyhock has built an international reputation as an educational retreat where leading thinkers and health practitioners come to teach workshops on healing, spiritual development and social change. The beachfront location on the southeast shore of Cortes is so magical that it in itself has led to life-changing experiences. Dana Bass Solomon, Hollyhock's CEO, remembers coming here with a girlfriend and walking down the road, with ocean and snow-capped mountains on one side and a sun-splashed forest on the other. "My friend said, 'You're in big trouble, this is the place you've always wanted to live.' I packed up my two kids, 12 and 16, and moved up."

Hollyhock has courses ranging from memoir writing to holistic health. Spiritual chanting, yoga and drumming workshops feed the physical needs and week-long meditative retreats sustain the spirit. There are a variety of bodywork sessions available as well as guided nature hikes and kayak trips.

Hollyhock is one of the largest employers on Cortes, providing about 85 seasonal jobs. In the spring and fall the Seeker program is open to artists who have projects to

Dianne Bersea in her studio on Cortes Island.
Dianne Bersea CSPWC AFCA photo

***Hollyhock Sanctuary* by Dianne Bersea.**
Dianne Bersea CSPWC AFCA photo

Right: A young woman begins the process for meditation at the Sanctuary, a cob structure at Hollyhock.

Below: Hollyhock has an international reputation for educational workshops that allow participants to explore new disciplines.

Bottom: The Hollyhock garden is a place of beauty as well as a source of fresh food.

work on. There is also a Karma Yoga program where participants can pay a nominal fee to stay for a month in exchange for volunteer work.

Many people want to teach at Hollyhock and it is program director Clare Day's job to vet submissions to make sure the material will resonate with workshop participants. She researches current trends, and plans for a 50/50 split between new and repeat programs. In keeping with Hollyhock's mission to inspire, nourish and support people who are making the world a better place, there is a social venture conference in the fall that brings entrepreneurs together to share business challenges.

King Karl's Castle

Cortes Bay on the southeast corner of the island is home to a five-storey castle with a dungeon, dining hall, eight bedrooms and three turrets. Karl Triller built the structure out of 13,000 cement blocks, a task that took him 12 years. He designed the castle and did most of the work himself, hauling buckets of cement up to the top turret with a rope and using a pony to drag logs up from the beach. At one time Karl would host banquets and have overnight guests in the castle but now that he is an elder statesman (he plays a king in the annual Cortes Day parade) the castle is open only for tours to day visitors.

Cortes Writer: June Cameron

June Cameron has written several notable books about growing up on Cortes and her adventures cruising the BC coast. After years of racing sailboats with all-women crews, she traded her sailboat for a powerboat on her 65th birthday. Now she lives in Cortes Bay with a miniature schnauzer that doubles as a canine doorbell since Cameron has hearing problems. Through the use of hearing aids, headphones for the TV and the internet she can cope quite well with her disability. Her grandfather had a homestead south of Cortes Bay and her family bought property on the north shore there, just behind the present Royal Vancouver Yacht Club outstation. The Seattle Yacht Club also has a large outstation in the south end of the bay not far from her house.

Cameron's social calendar starts off with a January potluck dinner (everyone is too busy at Christmas) and the spring oyster festival. In the summer she looks forward to Cortes Day at Smelt Bay Park, a day-long celebration with a parade, craft displays, food and kids' races.

Adventure Kayaking

Mike Moore offers tours of Mitlenatch Island and kayaking adventures with his 14-metre (46-foot) gaff-rigged fishing schooner. Compared to Quadra, which has a plethora of kayak companies, there are limited eco-tourism opportunities on Cortes. Moore graduated from the Canadian Coast Guard College and worked aboard different vessels before coming to Cortes in 1992, buying land and working as a kayak guide for a local company. He bought *Misty Isles*, a locally built fishing schooner, in 1998.

There is a leap of faith when you start a business. Taking a chainsaw to the fish hold, he removed the old boards and built bunks for four. In order to pass safety regulations for commercial passenger vessels he had to install sprinklers, escape hatches and myriad other safety modifications.

Licensed to carry 12 passengers, *Misty Isles* has a large wheelhouse that is perfect

Top: King Karl's castle, a five-storey cinder block building complete with a dungeon, turrets, dining hall and sleeping quarters.

Bottom: King Karl, a.k.a. Karl Triller, welcomes guests to his castle on Cortes Island.

for sheltering passengers on shoulder-season trips when the weather turns. On the large aft deck Moore can store up to nine kayaks when he is doing "mother ship" kayak trips. During those trips, the clients paddle all day and then Moore meets them with a hot dinner and all the amenities for a comfortable night's rest.

As with any true islander he supplements his summer income by taking on other jobs, running sail-training vessels in the fall and working as a naturalist-guide in the Antarctic during the winter.

Klahoose First Nation

The Squirrel Cove reserve at Tork is home to the band office and 46 members of the Klahoose Nation. Ken Brown was elected chief councillor in 2007 and since that time has worked hard to create jobs so that the 254 people living off-reserve can come home. The community plan has a layout for new subdivisions and construction has started on a 15,000-square-foot multi-purpose building that is being funded by forestry revenues.

Timber-cutting rights in the Toba Valley were recently transferred from corporate interests to the Klahoose First Nation, which Chief Brown considers a milestone in the band's history. Logging, forest management, supervision, booming and falling con-

Above: Captain Mike Moore teaches passengers aboard *Misty Isles* the finer points of navigation while sailing through Desolation Sound.

Right: *Misty Isles*, a 43-foot converted fishing schooner, is used as a charter vessel and mothership for kayaking adventures in and around Desolation Sound.

tracts are all undertaken by companies owned by Klahoose members. There is also a small milling program in Squirrel Cove using wood from the Toba River Valley. The lumber will be used in the new multi-purpose centre and in on-reserve housing projects. In terms of economic impacts, the First Nation hopes to cut 125,000 cubic metres (163,500 cubic yards) of timber in 2010, with an estimated value of $16 million.

Nearly forty band members are working at the Toba Inlet run-of-river power project being built by Plutonic Power and GE Energy Financial Services. A run-of-river project involves diverting water from a stream, through a powerhouse and back into the river. The generated power goes into the North American grid via a series of power lines.

Klahoose is the first band in BC to secure a sub-tidal geoduck tenure. Geoducks are large shellfish that live beneath the low-tide level of the ocean. They have been harvested commercially for years for Far Eastern markets and now that wild stocks are low they are being cultured. Chief Ken Brown has gone on the record about the importance of diverse business interests: "Right now it's important for First Nations, especially in our community, to start developing own-source revenue opportunities. Self-sufficiency, self-reliance and independence from government are what really strengthens communities and strengthens the sovereignty of the Klahoose First Nation."

Top left: The Squirrel Cove dock is quiet in the pre-dawn hour.

Above: The Klahoose people moved their principal village to Squirrel Cove on Cortes Island in the 1890s, relocating from isolated villages in Ramsay Arm, East and West Redonda Islands and Toba Inlet. Museum of Campbell River 17143

Left: The MV Aurora Explorer, a freight barge that takes passengers to remote parts of the coast, waits for high tide to unload logging equipment onto Elizabeth Island in Toba Inlet.

4

The Outer Islands

Marina Island

Situated off the southwest corner of Cortes Island, Marina Island was named by Spanish explorers after Hernán Cortés's mistress. The Royal Navy renamed it Mary Island in 1849 but it reverted to its original name in 1906.

The Marlatt family of Manitoba bought Marina Island in 1907 and built several homes. In 1910 the Chamadaska post office and telegraph station opened on the island and a 21-man crew was busy logging. Timber prices dropped when the economy slowed and the Marlatts sold to James Milne, a Scottish industrialist, in 1912. Milne left after a few years as he found island life too isolated. Today Shark Spit, a long sandy point in Uganda Passage, is a popular summer picnic spot and was once the venue for a party for the rich and famous. In the 1990s staff from Painter's Lodge were hired to cater a party held on the spit. Flowers were flown in from Hawaii and a local logger was contracted to load a generator onto his barge to provide power ashore. Georgina Little, one of the bar staff hired from Painter's, remembers setting up tables for eighty and tending a full-service bar. When the tide was out, there was a golf course on the beach with full perimeter security. Musicians Kenny G and David Foster played for the crowd, which included cell phone billionaires and KISS musician Gene Simmons. After a second party was held the media got curious so the venue was shifted to another private island the next year. Today, apart from picnickers and a few oyster farmers tending leases, the island is deserted.

Read Island

Read Island, between Quadra and Cortes, was named by Lt. Daniel Pender of the historic steamship *Beaver* for his naval colleague Captain William Viner Read. In 1883 logging camps started up on Read and in 1888 Edgar Wilmot Wylie arrived on the island. He had left the US under questionable circumstances and, soon after he built a hotel on the east coast of the island, was fined several times for selling alcohol to Natives. Two well-publicized murders on the island in the 1890s, graphically described

Above: The sea's natural bounty: clams and oysters from Marina Island.

Right: Brent Petkau's squatter shack on Marina Island where his family once lived while running oyster leases in the summertime.

UNDER REPAIR

by Jeanette Taylor in *Tidal Passages: A History of the Discovery Islands*, slowed settlement for a while. In the following years Read attracted such an interesting collection of settlers with so many different religious affiliations that it was hard to find a day of the week when they could all get together and socialize.

Charlie Rosen cleared a farm in 1910 next to the lake that bears his name and Robert Tipton, who later ran a store in Surge Narrows on the northwest side, paid the travel costs of six families so there would be enough students for a school in the late 1920s. The population hit a peak in the 1950s when there were about a hundred people living on the island. When Union Steamship stopped serving the island in the 1950s the population started a downward slide until the back-to-the-landers arrived in the 1970s.

Ralph and Lannie Keller started Coast Mountain Expeditions kayak lodge beside their Evans Bay home in the 1980s. They also opened Discovery Lodge at Surge Narrows, where they offer kayak and canoe rentals as well as bed and breakfast accommodation in the summer season.

A Taoist retreat was also operating in Evans Bay back in the 1980s. Silent Ground, or Quiet Dirt as the locals called it, was a spiritual retreat that was renowned for minimalist meals. Local tales abound about pale participants begging islanders to take them back to civilization for a square meal. There was also a herd of wild cows loose on the island about that time. The cows belonged to an islander who allowed them to roam free. One day a logger's door was left open by accident and the curious cows snuck into the cabin for a party that began when they knocked over the sooty chimney pipe. When the logger arrived the next weekend his only clue to the perpetrators were the meadow muffins halfway up the walls.

The island is gradually changing as retirees move full-time into what were once their recreational properties. Burton Wohl, a novelist and screenwriter, describes his time on Read Island in *Wolves, Whales and November Gales*. He writes lyrically about island life, its characters and keeping the proverbial woodpile stocked up, but he often retreated to Hollywood in the winter to work on screenplays. The population on Read is around eighty people these days but is getting older. An islander who came in the first back-to-the-land wave said the island needs another group of youthful settlers, but doubts they could afford the current land prices.

A scene not much removed from generations back, transportation via water and your best friend on board to share the ride.

Bottom left: The small outpost of Surge Narrows on Read Island has a post office and a school with a gym that serves as the unofficial community centre for dances and festivals.

Bottom: Bill Dutch, a Beaver floatplane pilot, waits for passengers embarking from Surge Narrows in the Discovery Islands.

Sonora Island

When the English and Spanish first surveyed the area in 1792 they mistakenly thought there was only one large island instead of three: Sonora, Maurelle and Quadra. Further surveys in the 1860s missed the Okisollo Channel separating Quadra from Maurelle. It was not until 1872 that Canadian surveyors, looking for a route for the transcontinental railway, detected the waterways separating the islands. It was this discovery that made the proposed railway unfeasible. Instead Burrard Inlet was chosen for the transcontinental terminus and the dream of a great metropolis on the Discovery Coast died.

Sonora's steep terrain and forested hillsides attracted loggers rather than farmers. Floating camps logged the bays along Okisollo Channel, there was a government forestry station up at Thurston Bay on the top of Sonora in the 1930s and around Owen Bay on the southeast shore was a thriving community with a school. Now, Owen Bay has only recreational properties and there are a few homesteads and fishing lodges on the east side of Sonora.

Ross Campbell and Fern Kornelsen live just south of Owen Bay in Diamond Bay, where they run a family eco-tourism business, Mothership Adventures, aboard the MV *Columbia III*. Their children grew up working on boats and hold multiple marine and kayak guide certifications. Older daughter Miray is the company administrator and her husband Luke Hyatt has his skipper's ticket as do the teenage twins Farlyn and Tavish.

The 21-metre (70-foot) *Columbia III* is well known up and down the coast, having served as a hospital ship for the Anglican Church's Columbia Coast Mission between 1956 and 1968. Mothership Adventures books a five-month season of trips with artists, photographers and writers along to lead workshops and tell the tales about the old coastal homesteads.

Ross and Fern lived in Whiterock Pass in 1974 and fell in love with the island life-

Above: Mothership Adventures come ashore to explore.

Right: MV *Columbia III* tied up at her home berth in Diamond Bay on Sonora Island.

style, buying property in Diamond Bay in late 1978. Before acquiring the *Columbia III* Campbell operated a tugboat and flew a commercial helicopter. He says that the people who have persevered in the outer islands have been resourceful and multi-talented, prepared to work hard for the simple life.

Sonora Resort

At first glance Sonora Resort could easily be mistaken for "Whistler in the Woods" because the resort resembles a small luxurious village in the wilderness. Accessible only by water or air, Sonora Resort was originally built by Mike Gallant, a Campbell River grocery store operator, as a high-end fishing resort. The Louie family, owners of the London Drugs and IGA chains, bought the resort in 2003 and embarked on an ambitious five-year building program. The wilderness resort joined the Relais & Châteaux world group of luxury hotels and gourmet restaurants in 2009. Attracting corporate and luxury travellers, the facility has 11 separate multi-room lodges that have floor-to-ceiling views over the Gillard Islands. One of the lodges, Sea Lion Pointe, is set on its own peninsula and highlighted with carvings and paintings from 11 top west coast artists.

Outdoor activities run from helicopter fly fishing and glacier picnics to salmon fishing and grizzly watching at nearby Orford River. There is a world-class spa, and guests can look forward to an unforgettable dining experience.

Sea Lion Pointe at Sonora Resort offers luxury accommodations in a wilderness setting.

Early morning vista on the longest day of the year at Sonora Resort.

Maurelle Island

Between Read and Sonora islands, Maurelle Island shares Sonora's rugged topography. Over the years there were only a few scattered homesteads and a small settlement of returned World War I soldiers at Antonia Point on the southwest tip.

Rob and Laurie Wood's house on a hill overlooking Okisollo Channel has been their home for the last thirty years.

Rob grew up in England mountaineering and when he came to the west coast to climb in the 1970s he bought a sailboat. While he was living on his boat in Vancouver's False Creek he met a cast of characters who were all being evicted due to a redevelopment scheme. "They'd bought this recently logged land on Maurelle and were desperate to find partners to pay $3,000 a share. I came up and looked at the place and fell in love with it. I met Laurie on a blind date in a pub in Squamish about the same time and invited her to come up and live on my boat."

Laurie went tree-planting every spring and Rob, who had trained as an architect in Britain, did design jobs for locals. Their lifestyle was simple, a tent platform morphed into a low-cost cabin and they built their present home with recycled bridge beams from Bute Inlet. Rob traded milling service for design services. Since they've never had a mortgage their lifestyle is flexible and versatile. Rob designed passive solar and heat sinks into the house, and a small Pelton wheel in the stream generates electricity to charge batteries for eight months of the year. Solar panels take up the slack in summer when stream flows are low. They have a big garden and buy staple foods in Campbell River.

Rob designed writer Hilary Stewart's house on Quadra, the Hansens' house on Sturt Island and did quite a bit of work at Hollyhock retreat centre. He never liked working indoors on sunny days so he and his wife got the idea of running an outdoor guiding business.

Wood-fired hot tub at Go with the Flow Adventures on Maurelle Island. Ian Douglas photo

The Woods ran Ocean to Alpine Adventure Travel through the 1990s. They guided two-week trekking and mountain-walking trips in Bute Inlet and Strathcona Park on Vancouver Island for a British travel agency. Although they enjoyed showing visitors the spectacular backcountry, eventually they stopped guiding trips as they found government regulations for commercial access too onerous.

Brody Wilson and Cristina Fox have started Go with the Flow Kayak Adventures in a cove just north of the Woods' property. They pulled a float house above high tide for a main house and have built a series of small cabins for kayak guests. Wilson grew up on Maurelle (his parents have a cabin not far from the Woods) and started kayak guiding when he was 18 so he knows the area intimately. Wilson and Fox have a young child who will undoubtedly grow up to feel as passionately about the coastal life as his parents.

Sturt Island: Living the Dream

Buying an island and spending your retirement homesteading on it for a dozen years is a dream for most of us. Kaare and Trudi Hansen live that dream.

From the moment they saw the island they fell in love with the big trees on Sturt, a small island located between Maurelle and Quadra at Surge Narrows. The Hansens bought the 34-hectare (85-acre) island then had two log cabins built in the Interior of BC, which were shipped down and re-assembled on the island. The log cabins became

**Kaare and Trudi
Hansen in their home
on Sturt Island.**
Ian Douglas photo

their home and guest house for seven years while a Quadra contractor worked on a larger post-and-beam house for them. The Hansens took over from lock-up and did all the interior finishing. Trudi laughed about the building phase of their life and the constant struggle with tides when bringing in building materials. "Whenever I saw a barge I would get a rash, worrying over whether they would get unloaded in time."

The main house, framed using old-growth fir beams recycled from a Port Alberni building, has a wall of windows looking down Hoskyn Channel and across to Quadra Island. They go to town about every ten to fourteen days to shop and try not to get stressed by ferry overloads. The trip to town can be a trial in the winter as wind storms drop trees across the Surge Narrows road and cause the ferry to Campbell River to cancel trips.

They have never had chickens or livestock but have watched a buck that was born on the island grow up over the last ten years. When summer comes the buck swims over to Read Island and in the fall, before the hunting season, it swims back. They know they have lived everyone's dream and have only one regret: "Maybe if we didn't build such a large house we could close things up and travel more."

Rendezvous Islands

The Rendezvous Islands are three islands located in Calm Channel between the north tip of Read and Raza Island. The north island has five full-time residents and twenty seasonal residents while the middle island has a small resort and six seasonal residents. South Rendezvous is a provincial park.

Karen and Pete Tonseth started Out of the Rain Adventures in 2007 on their 12-hectare (30-acre) property on North Rendezvous Island. They offer a destination kayak resort for people who want a bit of comfort after a day on the water. Four tent platforms with double beds and an outside seating area are situated along a woodland trail to maximize the views toward Whiterock Passage. Karen picked the charcoal-coloured Australian-made tents as they blend into the landscape. At one end of a trail is Bluff Cabin, a cozy day cabin where guests can relax and read by a wood stove. At the other end of the trail is the cedar shower building, with individual shower rooms for each tent and a separate composting toilet. Farther along the trail is the alfresco dining area.

Karen and Pete live in a boathouse that was originally built to house their kayaks. They are partnering with Go with the Flow Adventures on Maurelle Island so that guests can paddle with a guide from resort to resort. Karen looks after the day-to-day running of the resort and Pete is a radiologist who consults with patients in Australia over a satellite internet feed.

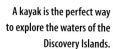

Kids mess about in boats as the sun sets on another summer day.

Growing Up on a Remote Island

by Jenn Kingstone, a young woman who grew up in the Discovery Islands

Twenty-seven years ago my parents brought me home from the hospital to North Rendezvous Island, a very small island north of Campbell River in the Discovery Islands. My parents had stumbled upon this wilderness paradise a few years before I was born, when sailing in the area. They had fallen in love with the beauty, remoteness, and the cheap land. The hippie, back-to-the-land movement was in full force, which may have helped my parents in their choice of location. Mum and Dad operated an oyster farm and at times Dad would work on nearby fish farms. My brother and I spent our childhoods being kids. This is such a simple idea, and yet when I look at city kids, I pity them in some ways. When I was ten, I couldn't care less about pop stars, clothing brands, and what car my parents owned. I was much more worried about building a bigger fort, or making a better trail through the woods. The island lifestyle did involve hard work on everyone's part. Whether it was getting the garden in during the spring, or harvesting it in the fall, or filling the woodshed with wood, we always had things to do. As life has taken me away from this existence and into a much more chaotic and messy one, I rely every day on the skills and knowledge I gained in my childhood. I am not alone in this; all of the kids that I grew up with are very similar. They also have their roots, which give them strength. The best gift that I have been given in my life from my parents has been the gift of this root, in this place.

A kayak is the perfect way to explore the waters of the Discovery Islands.

The Campbell River Area Looks Forward

With the great forest bonanza finally over and commercial fishing moribund, Campbell River and its region finds itself, like many BC resource communities today, having to rethink its place in the cosmos. It is not without options. Fish farming has become a major employer, mining will continue at least for a while and the forest industry will be heard from in the future. The Discovery Coast was an early entrant in the recreation economy, having achieved status as an international sportfishing destination by the 1890s and having served as the main access point for 250,000-hectare (625,000-acre) Strathcona Park with its fabulous system of lakes, rivers, waterfalls and alpine since 1911. The Discovery Islands and adjacent Desolation Sound have for some years been BC's most poplar cruising destination for pleasure boaters and this will only increase as the boating crowd ventures farther north and Campbell River's excellent services come into their own. Campbell River's traditional advantage as gateway to the surrounding hinterland continues, both to the islands and inlets of the mid-coast as well as the great inland spaces to the north and west. Not only does it perch astride the Island Highway leading to Port Hardy and points north, it sits at the beginning of scenic Highway 28 to Gold River and Tahsis, one of the main access routes to Vancouver Island's west coast.

Heading into the twenty-first century, Campbell River is a modern city that retains its traditional ties to British Columbia's coastal frontier. Perhaps nothing symbolizes its readiness to shape its own future so much as its impressive new downtown featuring the Discovery Harbour shopping centre, marina and cruise ship complex—fittingly owned by the area's first residents, the ever-enterprising Laichwiltach.

Following pages: A spectacular sunset over Stella Lake, north of Campbell River.

Aerial view of the Rendezvous Islands within Calm Channel. Toba Mountain is on the right and Stuart Island is directly behind the Rendezvous Islands.

5

Discovering Campbell River
and Discovery Islands

British Columbia Ferries' MV *Tenaka* seen from the air sailing the waters between Cortes and Quadra islands.

Getting Here

Situated on the east coast of central Vancouver Island, Campbell River is accessible by land, sea and air. BC Ferries has regular runs linking the British Columbia mainland to Vancouver Island. Campbell River is a one-hour drive from the Vancouver Island ferry terminal at Comox/Courtenay and two hours from the terminal at Nanaimo. The ten-minute ferry to Quadra Island leaves from downtown Campbell River. The ferry to Cortes Island leaves from Heriot Bay, a ten-minute drive across Quadra.

From Nanaimo, drivers have the choice of taking the scenic oceanside route (19A) or driving the four-lane, high-speed Inland Island Highway. Several airlines provide direct daily flights to Campbell River Airport and seaplanes provide services to the outer islands. There are various marinas with a range of amenities for boaters.

Transportation

BC Ferries (from Mainland to Vancouver Island and smaller local ferries): 1-888-223-3779 (toll-free within North America), 250-386-3431 (outside North America), *www.bcferries.com*

Campbell River Airport: 250-923-5012, *www.campbellriverairport.ca*

Bus: Campbell River Terminal: 250-287-7151

Waywest Water Taxi: 250-286-3050 *www.waywest.ca*

Corilair Air Charters: 250-287-8371 *www.corilair.com*

Black Ball Transport (ferry from Port Angeles, WA to Victoria, BC): 250-386-2202 (Victoria), 360-457-4491 (Port Angeles), *www.cohoferry.com*

Washington State Ferries: *www.wsdot.wa.gov/ferries/*

Victoria Clipper (passenger-only high-speed catamaran ferry service between Seattle, WA and Victoria, BC): Toll-free: 1-800-888-2535, Tel: 206-448-5000, *www.clippervacations.com*

A venerable Beaver floatplane, well known in the coastal region of British Columbia and around the world for its dependable service.

Accommodation

Accommodation runs from exclusive wilderness resorts such as Sonora Resort to renowned fishing lodges in Discovery Passage like Painter's and April Point. Tsa-Kwa-Luten Lodge is located on the sandy bluff at the south end of Quadra while the Heriot Bay Inn and Taku Resort are situated in the central part of the island. There are numerous B&Bs as well as several provincial and private campgrounds in the area. For more information, contact the various visitor info centres.

Contacts
Campbell River Visitor Centre: 877-286-5705 *www.visitorcentre.ca*
Quadra Island Visitor Info: 250-285-2058 *www.quadraisland.ca*
Cortes Island Visitor Info: *www.cortesisland.com*

Dining

Choices range from casual west coast fare in pub bistros and sushi bars to elegant dinners served on crisp white linens. The selection of local seafood includes oysters, clams, mussels, halibut, crab and prawns as well as several kinds of salmon.

Annual Events

Festivals and annual events in the area begin in March with Campbell River's literary festival **Words on the Water**. The **Cortes OysterFest** features fresh local seafood in the early part of May, and later in the month **Quadra's May Day**, which has been held annually on Rebecca Spit since 1898, has a maypole dance and parade. **Transformations on the Shore**, Campbell River's carving competition, and the **Quadra Island Art Studio Tour** occur in June. Campbell River celebrates **Canada Day** with a parade and fireworks, and during **Cortes Day** there is a small parade along with food and craft booths. The **North Island Logger Sports** held in August features log rolling and power saw competitions. There are fly-casting demonstrations and readings during the **Haig-Brown Festival** held in September along the banks of the river.

Angels on Horseback— oysters wrapped in bacon—hot off the grill at OysterFest.
Ian Douglas photo

Sea Lion Pointe at the five-star Sonora Resort represents the very finest in luxury accomodation and supports the largest collection of private artwork by local artists in British Columbia.

Downtown Campbell River

Campbell River Sportsplex is the premier recreation facility for Campbell River. It features outdoor sport fields as well as an indoor gymnasium and squash and racquet-ball courts. **Rotary Beach Park** is located north of Big Rock and just south of the 50th Parallel Marker. It is a popular picnic spot with a memorial garden and a sea-water wading lagoon.

The award-winning **Museum at Campbell River** is located across from the red **Torii Gate** in **Sequoia Park**. Just up the road is the **Centennial Park Outdoor Pool,** which is open from June to August. **Strathcona Gardens Recreation Complex** has a skating rink and indoor pool. The **Maritime Heritage Centre** close to the commercial harbour has a famous fishboat and on Sundays there is a **Farmers' Market** outside. Down by the Quadra ferry terminal is the First Nation **Heritage Pavilion** in Robert V. Ostler Foreshore Park. In the **Coast Discovery Marina** and the **Discovery Harbour Marina** there are wildlife and whale watching tours. The **Beaver Lodge Lands** has a series of popular hiking and biking trails. The **Haig-Brown House,** where Roderick and Ann raised their family on the banks of the Campbell River, is a B&B in the summer.

Above: A mother and daughter team creates crafts for the Pier Street Market held weekly at the Discovery Pier parking lot.

Right: An evening stroll on the Discovery Pier would not be complete without ice cream cones from the concession.

Seniors involved in the adaptive fitness program swim and workout at the Strathcona Gardens complex in Campbell River.

Campbell River Outskirts

The **Oyster River Nature Park** has a trail along the shoreline to the Salmon Point Pub. **Woodhus Slough** has a number of rare plants and almost two hundred bird species have been recorded here. **Storey Creek Golf Course** is locally owned and is rated one of the premier courses on the island.

Quinsam Campground is a provincial park/campground by the Quinsam River. In the springtime the riverside trails that lead up to the hatchery are carpeted with wildflowers, notably fawn and chocolate lilies. **The Canyon View Trail**, a popular 6-km (4-mi) walking circuit up and down the banks of the Campbell River, takes about an hour. The trail starts at the John Hart Powerhouse and continues across a footbridge to the north side of the river. **Elk Falls Park**, a day-use park, is home to Elk Falls, a 25-m (82-ft) vertical drop into a steep-walled canyon. There are massive old-growth Douglas fir and Sitka spruce by the trail leading to the falls. **McIvor Lake**, just outside of town, is a popular place to cool off with a swim. There are over 100 km of cross-country bike trails in the **Snowden Forest. Loveland Bay Provincial Park** on the shores of Campbell Lake has 31 sites.

Sun worshippers at McIvor Lake take in the scene, a popular summer destination for teen-agers and water sport enthusiasts

The **Ripple Rock Trail**, located 19 km (12 mi) north of Campbell River, takes about four hours to hike the 9.5-km (6-mi) long trail out to Seymour Narrows and back. Hikers venturing to the **Sayward** area can spend the day on the trail up **Mount H'kusam**, called Bill's Trail by the locals. The 8-hour return trip to the 1,604-m (5,261-ft) summit rewards hikers with sweeping views of the area, including the Village of Sayward, Kelsey Bay and the Salmon River estuary and wildlife reserve. **Mount Cain Ski Resort** is located southwest of Sayward, 25 minutes west off the Sayward Junction along Hwy 19. It's a 16-km (10-mi) drive on a gravel road from the highway to the day lodge (1,180 m/3,900 ft), with chains being mandatory on the last 10 km. Mount Cain offers a unique experience for skiers, snowboarders and backcountry explorers, with virtually no line-ups for lifts, and a friendly, welcoming atmosphere. The community-run Mount Cain is located in a regional park, and is ideal for families and snow enthusiasts of all skill levels. The Mount Cain resort usually opens from November to April. *www.mountcain.com*.

Backcountry skiing at Mt. Cain, Vancouver Island, British Columbia, Canada.

Expeditions and Fishing

Spirit of the West Adventures *www.kayakingtours.com,* **Coast Mountain Expeditions** *www.coastmountainexpeditions.com,* and **Mothership Adventures** *www.mothershipadventures.com* offer a variety of kayaking adventures. **Misty Isles Adventures** *www.mistyislesadventures.com* and **Sea Star Sailing** *www.islandsynergy.com* offer sailing adventures in the Discovery Islands.

A number of operators including **Knight Inlet Lodge, Discovery Marine Safaris, Campbell River Whale Watching** and **Aboriginal Journeys** offer whale-watching tours and grizzly-bear viewing. Check local listings.

The ***Aurora Explorer*** *www.marinelinktours.com* is a freight barge based out of Menzies Bay that takes passengers as it makes deliveries along the working coast.

Backcountry exploring: Strathcona Park, BC's oldest park, has a series of hiking trails and various peaks to climb.

The **Sayward Forest Canoe Route** takes three to four days to paddle and portage the 50-km (30-mi) route. The recommended direction to circumnavigate the route is counter-clockwise, commencing at any one of the numerous available starting points.

Down by the commercial harbour it's always fun to watch the action on the **public fishing pier**, which is open year-round. Comfortable saltwater **guide boats** are available through many lodges and there are **tyee rowboats** as well if visitors want to try their luck. There are freshwater fishing opportunities in the many lakes and rivers in the area. **Snorkel tours** down the Campbell River give visitors a chance to swim with the salmon.

Mothership Adventures tour arriving at Whaletown.

Thumbs-up after a very successful float down the Campbell River to view the salmon shooting upstream.

Quadra Island

In June 1996 the **HMCS *Columbia***, a former destroyer, was sunk just off Yellow Island by the Artificial Reef Society. The waters of Discovery Passage have a world-class reputation among coldwater divers because the strong currents mix the nutrient-rich waters to produce an abundance of marine life. The **Nuyumbulees Cultural Centre** at the Cape Mudge village has an important collection of potlatch masks and dance regalia. The **Tsa-Kwa-Luten Lodge** has overnight accommodation and jazz on Friday evenings. The **South End Farm Vineyard** is open for tasting tours. **Main Lake Park** is a popular canoeing destination with campsites around the lake and you can paddle through the narrows to Village Bay Lake. **Octopus Islands Marine Park** has protected anchorages and many boaters hike across the portage trail to **Small Inlet Park** where there is a trail up to Newton Lake. **Morte Lake Trail** is a popular hiking trail that is accessed by Walcan Road. Visitors can pick up a hiking trail map from most stores on the island. The view from **China Mountain** is well worth the 2-hour hike. **Rebecca Spit Marine Park** is a sheltered anchorage and popular picnic spot because of the long sandy beach. The **Quadra Island Golf Course** has nine holes under development but they are not playable until 2012.

Cortes Island

Ha'thayim Provincial Park is tucked away on the northwest coast of Cortes. On a hot summer day the anchorage is alive with laughter as kids scramble over the oyster-encrusted rocks discovering life in the tide pools. There are several trails over to **Squirrel Cove**, another popular anchorage, where there is a general store, craft store and restaurant by the government dock.

Kw'as Park trails are located in a 70-ha (173-ac) forested area between Gunflint and Hague Lake. The 12 km (7.5 mi) of trails pass through areas of virgin old-growth and second-growth Douglas fir along with bluffs covered by pine, arbutus and manzanita. In the 1920s the area was logged using a steam donkey to pull fallen timber into Gunflint. The logs were floated down Hague Lake and sluiced down a creek into Manson's Lagoon.

Gorge Harbour Marina has a fuel dock, a pool, store, accommodation and RV sites. **Mansons Landing Provincial Park** has a sandy spit and visitors can walk up for a refreshing swim in nearby **Hague Lake Provincial Park**. **Smelt Bay Provincial Park** on the south end of the island has 23 campsites and is the site for the annual **Cortes Day**.

Top: This folky building can be found amongst the Octopus Islands.

Bottom: Cortes Beach.

Author's Acknowledgements

Ian would like to thank fellow author Jeanette Taylor for her help and encouragement throughout the project. Keith and Shelly, Jon and Susi kindly helped with many meals while the writer was in residence. The following people were also gracious with their stories and time:

Alan, Valerie and Mary Haig-Brown; Amber Stowe; Annette Yourke; Bill and Mark Henderson; Bill Dutch; Bill O'Connor; Blair Maclean; Brian Sharpe; Cec Robinson; Charlie Cornfield; Chief Ken Brown; Chief Pollard; Chief Richard Harry; Clare Day; Daisy Sewid; Dale Anderson; Dan Samson; Dana and Joel Solomon; David Rousseau; Diana and Connie Kretz; Dianne Bersea; Donna Bracewell; Emma Douglas; Erika Grundman; Erin Pierce; Frank Assu; Greg Osoba; Harper Graham; Irene Blueth; Jack Innis; Jacquie Gordon; Jocelyn Reekie; John Grant; John Woodward; Joy Inglis; Judith Wright; June Cameron; Kaare and Trudi Hansen; Karl Triller; Ken Mar; Len Ring; Linda Inrig; Lorna Brown; Margaret Nyland; Mark Murphy; Marnie Andrews; Mary McIntosh; Michael Mascall; Mike Gage; MJ Crawley; Murray Ambercrombie; Myna Boulding; Norberto Rodriguez; Quentin Dodd; Ralph and Lannie Keller; Richard and Michelle Glickman; Rob and Laurie Wood; Roger McDonnel; Ron Neufield; Ross Campbell & Fern Kornelsen; Sandy Spearing; Steve and Carol London; Sue Ellingsen; Thor Peterson.

Photographer's Note

The success in obtaining images for a project of this magnitude is largely dependent on the ability of the photographer to access areas and situations that provide the best photographic opportunities. To that end, I would like to thank all those folks who were instrumental in helping me with this project: Corilair for the aerials; Marine Link Tours; Western Forest Products; Hollyhock; Ross and the MV *Columbia III*; Misty Isles charters; Campbell River Heritage Centre; and Sonora Resort. And to all I photographed in my travels throughout Campbell River, Quadra Island and the Discovery Islands, I thank you; it is to you that this book is dedicated. I would also be remiss in not acknowledging my wife, Heather, and my children, Josh and Megan, for their patience and understanding in allowing me to do what I do.

Boomer Jerritt
Strathcona Photography
Email: strathconaphoto@shaw.ca
Website: *www.strathconaphotography.com*

Suggested Reading

Andersen, Doris. *Evergreen Islands: The Islands of the Inside Passage: Quadra to Malcolm.* Sidney, BC: Gray's Publishing, 1979.

——. *The Columbia is Coming!* Sidney, BC: Gray's Publishing, 1982.

Assu, Harry, with Joy Inglis. *Assu of Cape Mudge: Recollections of a Coastal Indian Chief.* Vancouver, BC: UBC Press, 1989.

Baikie, Wallace. *Rolling with the Times.* Campbell River, BC: Kask Graphics, 1985.

Blanchet, M. Wylie. *The Curve of Time.* Vancouver, BC: Whitecap Books, 1990, c1968.

Bown, Stephen R. *Madness, Betrayal and the Lash: The Epic Voyage of Captain George Vancouver.* Vancouver, BC: Douglas & McIntyre, 2008.

Cameron, June. *Destination Cortez Island: A Sailor's Life along the BC Coast.* Surrey, BC: Heritage House, 1999.

Douglas, Gilean. *The Protected Place.* Sidney, BC: Gray's Publishing, 1979.

Egan, Van Gorman. *River of Salt: Tyee Fishing in Discovery Passage.* Campbell River, BC: Kask Graphics, 2004.

Harbord, Heather. *Desolation Sound: A History.* Madeira Park, BC: Harbour Publishing, 2007.

Harrington, Sheila, and Judi Stevenson, eds. *Islands in the Salish Sea: A Community Atlas.* Surrey, BC: Touchwood Editions, 2005.

Isenor, D.E., E.G. Stephens and D.E. Watson. *Edge of Discovery: A History of the Campbell River District.* Campbell River, BC: Ptarmigan Press, 1989.

Lebowitz, Andrea, and Gillian Milton. *Gilean Douglas: Writing Nature, Finding Home.* Victoria, BC: Sono Nis, 1999.

Mitchell, Helen. *Diamond in the Rough: The Campbell River Story.* Langley, BC: Frontier Publishing, 1975.

Reekie, Jocelyn, and Annette Yourk, eds. *ShoreLines: Memoirs & Tales of the Discovery Islands.* Quathiaski Cove, BC: Kingfisher Publishing, 1995.

Taylor, Jeanette. *River City: A History of Campbell River and the Discovery Islands.* Madeira Park, BC: Harbour Publishing, 1999.

——. *Tidal Passages: A History of the Discovery Islands.* Madeira Park, BC: Harbour Publishing, 2008.

——. *The Quadra Story: A History of Quadra Island.* Madeira Park, BC: Harbour Publishing, 2009.

Taylor, Jeanette, and Ian Douglas. *Exploring Quadra Island: Heritage Sites & Hiking Trails.* Quathiaski Cove, BC: Fernbank Publishing, 2001.

Tovell, Freeman. *At the Far Reaches of Empire: The Life of Juan Francisco de la Bodega y Quadra.* Vancouver, BC: UBC Press, 2008.

Wild, Paula, with Rick James. *The Comox Valley: Courtenay, Comox, Cumberland and Area.* Madeira Park, BC: Harbour Publishing, 2006.

Williams, Judith. *Clam Gardens: Aboriginal Mariculture on Canada's West Coast.* Vancouver, BC: New Star Books, 2006.

Index

For my parents, who encouraged my spirit of adventure.
—Ian Douglas

Harbour Publishing Co. Ltd.
P.O. Box 219, Madeira Park, BC, V0N 2H0
www.harbourpublishing.com

Cover photographs by Boomer Jerritt
Edited by Peter Robson
Index prepared by Natalia Cornwall
Cover design by Teresa Karbashewski
Text design and maps by Roger Handling, Terra Firma Digital Arts
Printed and bound in Canada

Harbour Publishing acknowledges financial support from the Government of Canada through the Canada Book Fund and the Canada Council for the Arts, and from the Province of British Columbia through the BC Arts Council and the Book Publishing Tax Credit.

Library and Archives Canada Cataloguing in Publication

Douglas, Ian, 1954-
        Campbell River : gateway to the Inside Passage : including Strathcona, the Discovery Islands and the mainland inlets / Ian Douglas ; photos by Boomer Jerritt.

Includes index.
ISBN 978-1-55017-501-1

        1. Campbell River (B.C.)—History. 2. Campbell River (B.C.)—Biography. 3. Campbell River (B.C.)—Pictorial works. 4. Campbell River Region (B.C.)—Pictorial works. I. Jerritt, Boomer II. Title.

FC3849.C35D68 2010   971.1'2   C2010-904399-5